The Freedom Manifesto

Praise for Karan Bajaj's Books

Shortlisted for the Crossword Book Pick of the Year
Shortlisted for the Golden Quill Award
Shortlisted for the Teacher's Achievement Award
Shortlisted for India Today's 35 Under 35 Achievers-Artist

'A beautifully rendered epic journey. Transcendent yet readable, spiritual yet wildly and deliberately accessible, the book works on many levels and excels at them all.'

—*New York Journal of Books*

'A racy and entertaining account of a romp through an ever-changing yet timeless India. Wild, Witty and Wicked!'

—Ruskin Bond

'Karan Bajaj weaves a modern day epic you simply will not forget. He writes clean, simple prose that zips so fast you'll forget you're reading. He transcends his outlet and sends his creative heart directly into yours. Incredible.'

—Neil Pasricha, *New York Times* bestselling author of *The Happiness Equation* and *The Book of Awesome*

'Upon finishing this book, you will likely find yourself asking the big questions. You may also find yourself selling your possessions, dusting off your passport, quitting your job, and buying a one-way ticket to the end of the earth. Karan Bajaj has written a compelling adventure, with vivid settings, meaty themes, and a satisfying conclusion.'

—Jonathan Evison, author of *The Revised Fundamentals of Caregiving*

'An amazing journey. Wonderful characters who keep you hooked till the very end.'

—Rajkumar Hirani, director, *Munnabhai M.B.B.S.*, *3 Idiots*

'Pacy, unpretentious and great fun to read.'

—*Outlook India*

'A taut, gripping saga with the manic pace of an action film.'

—*Hindustan Times*

'Not for the weak-hearted! A candid representation of the lives of extraordinary people who take the road less traveled. Evokes a sense of awe so does the simplicity of language and the lucid writing style of the author.'

—*Deccan Herald*

The Freedom Manifesto

7 Rules to Live the Life of Your Calling

Karan Bajaj

HARPER BUSINESS

An Imprint of HarperCollins *Publishers*

First published in hardback in India by Harper Business 2022
An imprint of HarperCollins *Publishers*
4th Floor, Tower A, Building No 10, DLF Cyber City,
DLF Phase II, Gurugram, Haryana – 122002
www.harpercollins.co.in

This edition published in paperback in India
by HarperCollins *Publishers* 2024

2 4 6 8 10 9 7 5 3 1

P-ISBN: 978-93-6213-446-2
E-ISBN: 978-93-5629-253-6

Typeset in 10.5/14 Berling LT Std at
Manipal Technologies Limited, Manipal

Printed and bound at
Thomson Press (India) Ltd

'Make mistakes of ambition, not mistakes of sloth.'

—Machiavelli

'I must only warn you of one thing. You will become a different person in the course of these years. For that is what the art of archery means: a profound and far-reaching contest of the archer with himself. Perhaps you have hardly noticed it yet but you will feel it very strongly when you meet friends and acquaintances again in your own country; things will no longer harmonize as before. You will see with different eyes and measure with different measures. It has happened to me too, and it happens to all who are touched by the spirit of the art.'

—Eugen Harrigel, Zen in the Art of Archery

'Hard choices, easy life. Easy choices, hard life.'

—Jerzy Gregorek

Contents

Introduction
Your Path to Freedom

FIRST, sit in a quiet place.

Now, close your eyes and visualize your ideal life ten years from now.

Don't worry, this isn't a wishful exercise to manifest your dreams. Instead, we're taking the first practical step to articulate your deepest, most personal goals. The hard work required to achieve your goals will come next.

For now, don't put any constraints on your thinking. Just be *as specific as possible* in visualizing your ideal life ten years from now, while asking yourself these three questions:

1. Where do you wake up in the morning ten years from now? What is the view from your room?
2. You're getting ready for the day. Where do you go to work? Whom are you working with? What are you working on?
3. Do you have a partner? If so, who are they? Do you have children?

Then, write down your answers.

Now, look at them. How did you visualize your perfect life? The underlying theme in these answers is your dharma, or your deepest natural tendency. In Buddhism and Vedic philosophy, every living being has a dharma, a natural instinct they can't help but express. A tree grows and bears fruit. The river flows and enriches hundreds. They aren't trying to do good or bad, they aren't debating pros and cons, they're just helpless to act as they are.

You can only feel whole if you're true to this natural thrust.

No financial gain, no material accomplishment can compensate for a life not lived in accordance with this natural law.

Ten years ago, in 2012, when I'd done this exercise, I'd visualized three things:

1. I wake up in the mountains or somewhere surrounded by greenery.
2. I create something with complete independence, like a book or my own company, and my work has a profound impact on the world.
3. I have a small family.

Back then, I had none of these in my life. I was living in New York City, in a studio apartment with windows facing a parking lot. I'd written two novels by the time, *Keep Off the Grass* (2008) and *Johnny Gone Down* (2010), published by HarperCollins India, but neither had been published internationally to allow me to become a full-time writer. My corporate job of marketing processed food at Kraft felt devoid of meaning and impact as my interest in yoga and meditation grew. And I was single at thirty-three, feeling I was too far from my ideal life to settle down.

I had to change my work to change my destiny. For the next ten years, I pursued my thrust for independence and impact—although nothing worked initially. Shortly after doing this exercise, I left my job to become a full-time writer. I set out to write a novel that I thought would inspire millions. The book, *The Seeker,* was rejected sixty-one times by agents and publishers. I kept revising the manuscript daily for three years until it was finally accepted by Penguin Random House worldwide for publication in 2016. There was to be no redemption in publishing though. Despite the publisher's high expectations for the book, it sold such few copies that excess printed copies had to be pulped. With no money coming in from the book, in order to keep writing full time, I set up a passive income stream with online courses to support my writing. The courses lost money, dipping further into my fast-dwindling savings.

I took up a job once again in late 2016 but was restless to build things of meaning again, so I left in 2019 to start WhiteHat Jr, an education technology company with a lofty mission of making every kid in this world a creator. My family thought I was reckless for not having a stable job when I was almost forty years old. One day at a dinner, just when I was starting the company, a close relative told me that he'd never want his children to grow up to be like me, unwilling to stop drifting in adulthood. The remark hit me hard. I knew the odds were heavily stacked against me becoming a tech entrepreneur. I was too old, my finances were stretched with two young children in school and given the failure rate of 90 per cent for start-ups, I was likely to fail again. When would I end my Faustian quest? Should I give up the dream and settle down?

But you can't be whole until you pursue your dharma.

I wanted to build things that would have a large impact on the world. Nobody said it would be easy. I started WhiteHat Jr in November 2018 with the mission of making every child in the world a creator, and in August 2020, BYJU's, the world's largest education technology organization, acquired the company for $300 million. On the surface, WhiteHat Jr's start-up to exit took less than two years, but the seeds were planted a decade ago when I first committed to pursue a life of independence and impact after doing the exercise I shared earlier in this chapter.

What is your dharma, your natural thrust, your innate tendency?

Did you visualize financial independence, the most fundamental of the soul's cries, so that you can be liberated to pursue your calling? Or did you envision having a large impact on the world? In both cases, the next few pages will give you a step-by-step guide to reach your goals. In Part I, you'll learn the seven rules to radically transform your mindset to an owner's mindset today. I wish I'd known these rules when I started on the path to independence, to save me from crippling self-doubt and indecisiveness, which come from wanting to follow your own path and no one around you being supportive of it.

1. The 4 Per Cent Rule: Your Exact Freedom Goal
2. Net Impact Rule: Multiply Your Net Impact to Multiply Your Net Worth

3. Salary/14 Lakh Quitting Rule: How and When to Quit Your Job
4. '30x7' Ownership Shift: The One Mindset Shift for Freedom
5. Daily '1/1/1' Routine: Maximize Your Energy with one Proven Routine
6. The '90 Per Cent Failure/100 Per Cent Learning' Rule: Increasing Your Ownership Success Probability
7. '50/30/20' Investing Rule: Your Freedom Investing Playbook.

Part II will give you specific, detailed guidelines with exact tools, from email templates to job descriptions, to solve the most common problems you'll face when you create things independently.

1. **Start-up Starter Kit Number 1:** How to Find Your Game-Changing Ownership Idea
2. **Start-up Starter Kit Number 2:** How to Raise Funding with No Product
3. **Start-up Starter Kit Number 3:** How to Write a Successful Pitch Desk
4. **Start-up Starter Kit Number 4:** How are Companies Valued?
5. **Start-up Starter Kit Number 5:** How to Start Up with No Co-founder
6. **Start-up Starter Kit Number 6:** How to Find Product Market Fit Fast
7. **Start-up Starter Kit Number 7:** How to Scale a Company: Three Tools That Work

Combine Parts I and II to start your journey of freedom and impact today. Each word here comes from my lived experience and hence is practical enough to implement immediately. There is no empty motivation here, just a step-by-step reality of what it'll take for you to break the shackles of convention to live a life of your calling. My only goal is to light a path which I wish someone had lit for me when I made a bid for freedom and kept experiencing the hopelessness of defeat. You'll experience failure too. Only you'll know that there'll be light at the end, and your journey will light the way for other journeys.

My greatest joy is in seeing this cycle be perpetuated so that more people live their dharma and make the world better by expressing their best selves in it.

Only Growth Decisions: Seven Exercises for Seven Rules

In between my ownership ventures, when I was Discovery Communications' India head, I was outside the Bharatiya Janata Party's (BJP) head office in New Delhi in July 2018. The prime minister's team had just greenlit Narendra Modi's presence in *Man vs Wild with Bear Grylls,* Discovery's global flagship show. His participation was a major coup for Discovery in India. Bear Grylls, the popular British survivalist, had been trying to do a show in India for more than a decade, but no one had been able to make the logistics work. Now, he'd be paired with a globally recognized leader, making this among select non-fiction television shows from India to be exported around the world. Outside the office, my team congratulated me. They'd never thought he would agree, but I'd been persistent in following up. This could be the event of the year for Indian television. My career was going places. I should've been exhilarated. Instead, I felt the same nervous energy I'd felt many times before, when I was not living my destiny. My time here was up.

The next week, I gave my notice to Discovery.

I'd given my all to expand Discovery in India for almost three years, creating new local content, launching television channels, striking digital partnerships and finally getting the premier of the country on the network. But now, I had to follow my calling once again. I wanted to pursue a life of independence and impact and take another chance at building something meaningful from scratch, this time a technology start-up, even though I knew very little about technology and had no co-founder. My heart sank at how high the odds of things not working out were.

But there are only two decisions—decisions of growth and decisions of fear. I'd deepened so much from my growth decisions—whether it was leaving Procter & Gamble to backpack in South America and eastern Europe for six months in 2008, taking a sabbatical to learn yoga and meditation for a year in 2013 or becoming a full-time writer in 2015—that I'd never regretted the decisions, even when they didn't work out. In contrast, I felt I had wasted eighteen months of my life when I took a decision out of fear, to stick to management consulting at Boston Consulting Group in 2009 even though I was a misfit for the job. I'd been worried about how my résumé would look to prospective employers if I left within six months. Staying longer out of fear was a mistake. I saw great value in the work but was too much of a hands-on operator to personally enjoy spending all my time doing analyses and making presentations, so I was miserable for most of my time there. My world had shrunk to thinking only about my problems, and a part of me went numb. And eventually, I left the company anyway. I don't think I strengthened my résumé by not having my full heart in something.

Always make decisions of growth versus fear/worry/what people will say/how résumés will look.

Growth opens new avenues. Fear contracts your life.

The seven rules in this book are accompanied by one exercise each. Choose growth versus fear when you do the exercises. Your first move may not work out, as in my case, nor your second. But you'll enter a stream of bold actions with your first step, which has genius, power and magic in it, which'll eventually lead to freedom.

PART I

The 7 Rules for Freedom

'I was never a petty thief. I wanted the whole world or nothing at all.'

—Charles Bukowski

1

The 4 Per Cent Rule

Your Exact Freedom Goal

SIX years into my first job at Procter & Gamble in 2008, I felt increasingly suffocated by the daily, predictable rhythm of a corporate job. The company was great, but I couldn't muster the passion to grow a few points of market share for a laundry detergent or a shampoo every day.

I didn't know whether I wanted to work in a different industry or profession, so I decided to quit my job to go backpacking across South America and eastern Europe for six months.

My family was appalled by this decision when I told them the day before I told my boss. I was twenty-eight at that time. My mother felt I was shamelessly evading responsibility by not getting married and having children, as my sister had done at my age and my cousins were doing then. 'You can't act like an American when you're from India,' she said. The next day, my manager requested me to reconsider. He reminded me that Procter & Gamble was a one-way door. Once I left, I would never be taken back. Why did I want to self-destruct after a promising start to my career, having been promoted fast and given a rare chance to move from India to the US?

My throat tightened. I had few rational explanations for either my mother or my boss. One reason for my restlessness was my rootless childhood. My father was in the Indian Army, so while growing up we kept changing schools every couple of years as he was transferred from one army base to another. By the twelfth grade, I had changed nine schools. Now, in adulthood, I craved change, whether in the places where I lived or in the relationships I built, and was restless when life settled into a routine.

Another explanation was the growing independence that came out of my move from India to the US with Procter & Gamble two years earlier. I had moved to Cincinnati at a time when few expatriates lived there. For the first time in my life, I had nothing to do and no one to visit on long, cold weekends. I would often feel desperately lonely, so I filled my time by reading avidly, hiking in the nearby mountains and writing a novel. The less I was surrounded by people, the more authentic I became to myself. And some instinct was guiding me that it was time to leave my comfort zone and experience more of the world. I'd always dreamt of crossing the Amazon from Brazil to Peru by boat and seeing the Inca ruins at Machu Picchu. If not now, when? If not me, who? I had to take the plunge.

It was a romantic decision. And it turned out to be a terrible one—at least in the short term.

I left Procter & Gamble in March 2008 at the peak of the US economic boom and came back in September

2008 on the same day the Lehman Brothers collapsed. The US economy crashed during the financial crisis and all jobs dried up. I'd used up all my savings in six months of backpacking across South America and eastern Europe. So I lived on a couch at my sister's home in Gaithersburg, Maryland, a suburb of Washington, DC. My friends from business school at the Indian Institute of Management, Bangalore (IIM-B), and engineering at the Birla Institute of Technology (BIT), Mesra, most of whom were entering their thirties, were sharing pictures of their first houses and their newborns.

And I was single, jobless and dead-broke at the age of twenty-nine.

Why did I leave my secure job to travel aimlessly around the world?

I applied frantically to any job that would take me anywhere in the country, and landed an entry-level role in management consulting. This job was for freshers out of business school and would set me back by six years in my career. But I had no option then. One after the other, I was rejected for all mid-level roles in brand marketing. No one was hiring during the recession, especially someone whom they perceived as not knowing the US culture well, since I'd spent only two years in the US. Once, I travelled for a full day by Greyhound bus from my sister's place for an interview with a paint company in the middle of Illinois for a brand manager position. I thought it would be easier to get the job since few people would want to live away from metropolitan cities in their early career, but I was rejected for my lack of US experience there as well. I started the management consulting role so that I could leave my sister's couch and pay for my own rental apartment. But I was so shaken by hitting rock bottom that I vowed to never take a major risk again.

The economy opened up again in two years. I changed jobs from Boston Consulting Group and joined Kraft as senior brand manager, a more appropriate position for my experience. Soon, I started to appreciate how much I'd grown from the six months of backpacking. I'd returned with a more boundary-less view of the world, which shaped all my decisions after, from my life partner being American to moving to New York so that I would be surrounded with more diverse views. *Johnny Gone Down*, the novel I'd conceptualized during the travel, became a bestseller with a significant movie deal. I couldn't draw a direct correlation between my sabbatical and my career, but I did well at Kraft, getting promoted from senior brand manager to director and then to senior director within three years, a record of sorts. My first deep brush with joblessness and failure had made me more mature and calm. I was a better leader than I'd been before. Over time, I didn't regret my six-month sabbatical. I'd grown in unexpected ways—and the world was rewarding the growth.

In 2012, four years after my first sabbatical, I was pulled to the road again, this time to learn yoga and meditation in India. My mother died of cancer in 2010. Her body had withered away over two years as the disease spread from her ureter to her bones. She was just fifty-six and went from a tall, authoritative presence to a shrivelled yellow skeleton on a wheelchair. Her painful death brought my meaning-of-life questions to the forefront: Why does a human suffer? Who determines this cycle of birth and death? I'd always been drawn to Buddhism and Indian spiritual texts like the Bhagavadgita and the Upanishads, but now my quest became more urgent. I had done a basic yoga and meditation practice, but felt I had to go much deeper to get a direct, mystical experience into the nature of reality. Kerry, my then girlfriend and now wife, and I decided to leave our jobs to travel for a year in late 2012. We planned to go backpacking from Europe to India by road over three months, using the cheapest modes of transport—walking, bus or boat—and staying in youth hostels and train stations along the way, practising the stoic idea of wilful poverty. If you can train your soul to understand how little you need to live joyfully, you'll live a life of the spirit, unhindered by constant pursuit of more material acquisitions. In India, we'd stay for six months, first at Sivananda Ashram in Madurai, Tamil Nadu, to deepen our yoga practice by doing a structured yoga teacher's training course, followed by learning meditation in various ashrams in the Indian Himalayas. On our return, I planned to stay at the Obras artists' retreat in Estremoz, a Portuguese village, to write my third novel. This time, we did better financial planning. I budgeted Rs 10 lakh for the trip, then added six months of living expenses in New York while I found a job after I returned, and further, added six months of buffer expenses to ensure I didn't land on my sister's couch again if I was unlucky enough to come back during another global recession. I was nervous about leaving my job again but deep down, I understood that I wouldn't grow as much by spending one more year doing the same things in my job as I would by taking this leap of personal transformation. I had to take a chance again.

The sabbatical went as planned through 2012 and 2013. Once again, I grew tremendously from the trip. My energy levels shot up from the daily yoga practice, improving my output at work on return. I felt calmer and more still with meditation. My writing deepened from the full-time focus in the artists' retreat, and I planned to submit the novel I was still working on, *The Seeker*, for international publication, for the first time. Everything was on track, except that the return was even harder than the first time.

I was fortunate to get a job back in Kraft Foods in late 2013 immediately after our sabbatical, six months ahead of my expectations. My finances were secure but I hadn't planned for how much I would change spiritually from the sabbatical. Kraft was a great organization, but I felt a growing unease with marketing processed food when my own diet was turning fully natural with my heightened awareness of the body's anatomy from my yoga teacher's training. The daily excesses of the US—big houses, multiple cars, expensive restaurants—were jarring after months of sleeping daily on hard beds in ashram dormitories and taking cold showers. I wanted to quit my job to write and leave New York City to live in nature. Neither looked possible. Kerry and I had just got married. We both wanted kids. How do you have it all? How do you pursue a life of your highest calling while still having a family?

I wasn't conventionally materialistic and had always shunned buying houses, cars, any kind of material assets. So I'd never dreamt of accumulating money. I'd also liked my corporate brand-management career until then. You worked on packaging design and television advertising to grow a brand's market share, while deeply analysing consumption and competitive data. It was a perfect mix of creativity and analytics, a rare exception among the mostly left-brained careers after business school. But now, I had turned weary of consumerism. For the first time, I questioned the script. Would I always have to work in a job I didn't feel deeply for? How would I pursue my interests in writing and spirituality along with kids? I understood now that money was a tool for spiritual growth rather than material acquisition. Having just enough money to meet your family's basic needs could liberate you to follow your creative and spiritual longing. My need for financial freedom was suddenly urgent.

How much money was enough to be free?

I couldn't find a straight answer.

Then, I discovered the **4 per cent rule** for financial freedom.

It changed my life.

The 4 Per Cent Rule

I came across the 4 per cent rule as a guideline for American retirees to manage their net worth after retirement,[1] but the more I dug in, iterating with my own analyses, I realized that the exact principles work for everyone, whether you're seventy-five years old or thirty-five years old:

> Your target net worth for financial freedom = (Your projected annual expenses)/(4 per cent)

First, determine the all-in annual expenses you'll need to live a life aligned to your values. Include your housing costs, transportation, utilities, groceries, insurances, kids' school fees, travel and entertainment, everything.

Now, divide this number by 4 per cent or 0.04.

The result is your target net worth to achieve financial freedom.

4% RULE

For instance, if your projected all-in annual expenses are Rs 50 lakh per year, then your target net worth = Rs 12.5 crore.

You're free to live your calling the moment you hit Rs 12.5 crore.

Free. Liberated. Done.

You may still go to your job daily if that's your dharma. But you don't have to. You can live off your savings for the rest of your life, no matter your age, and spend every moment in pursuit of your highest calling.

Four per cent is your trigger to live a life perfectly in accordance with your dharma.

Rationale of the 4 Per Cent Rule

You'll generate a guaranteed 4 per cent annual net return on your net worth if you invest your principal amount in stable, conservative assets.

For example, if you'd invested passively any time in the last two decades in the Bombay Stock Exchange Sensitive Index (BSE Sensex), which is an aggregation of thirty well-established and financially stable companies, like Hindustan Lever and Asian Paints, your ten-year rolling return for the twenty-year period from 2002 to 2021 would've been 12.26 per cent.[2] The ten-year average rolling return simply means average of returns for each of the ten-year periods starting from 2002–12, 2003–13 and so on till 2011–21.

Now let's add dividend yields, while adjusting (subtracting) for inflation and taxes:

12.26 per cent (BSE Sensex ten-year rolling return)
+ 1.37 per cent (rolling dividend yield for the same ten-year period)
– 7.62 per cent (India's average rolling inflation rate)
– Maximum possible tax on capital gains from equity and dividends

= **4.04 per cent net return**

You don't need to be an extraordinary investor to get the moderate 4 per cent net return; anyone can get these returns by simply investing passively in index funds like BSE Sensex or BSE 500.[3] And these are your worst-case returns. In all likelihood, your net return will be higher with better tax planning on equity and dividend capital gains.

You'll see the same phenomenon in the US.[4]

7.45 per cent (S&P 500 ten-year rolling return)
+ 2.01 per cent (rolling dividend yield for the same ten-year period)
– 1.95 per cent (average rolling inflation rate in the US)
– Maximum possible tax on capital gains from equity and dividends

= **5.62 per cent net return**

Here, S&P 500 represents 500 mature, publicly traded companies. Again, you'll get higher than 4 per cent annual net returns in every decade if you invest passively in S&P 500 index funds or Dow Jones.

In fact, the average three-year, five-year, seven-year, ten-year or even fifteen-year rolling returns for the twenty-year period between 2002 and 2021, for major stock indices of both India and the US, have been more than 4 per cent after inflation indexing and adjusting for taxes.[5]

The 4 per cent rule always works. You can, therefore, live off the returns of your investments every year if you budget to live within 4 per cent of your net worth. In rainy years, where you have either unforeseen high-expense events, like travel or health issues, or equity markets crash from events like COVID-19, you draw upon the principal amount and replenish it again when the markets improve.

Your projected expenses divided by 4 per cent is your golden net worth target for freedom.

My 4 Per Cent Story

I did the 4 per cent exercise in 2014, during my desperate times after our yoga sabbatical. I'd feel most suffocated in my daily ninety-minute commute from Brooklyn where I lived to the Kraft office in East Hanover, New Jersey, as I crossed industrial towns and passed billboards announcing new television shows, while deeply missing the snow-capped Himalayas where we had lived barely a year ago. I heard a version of the 4 per cent rule in one of the many self-help podcasts I listened to during the commute. A weight lifted off my shoulders after I did the exercise.

Now, I had a goal to chase, however unattainable it seemed then.

I set our projected annual expenses at Rs 1 crore per year. We could live on much less, but I projected conservatively into a future where our kids would go to college and our elderly parents would need medical help.

Our target net worth was, therefore, Rs 25 crore.

Next, I projected how much time we would take to get there if we continued our current jobs and expenses, using the following assumptions:

- Current salary (Y0): Rs 1.5 crore per year (USD salary converted to INR as I was living in the US then)
- Average savings: 20 per cent annually
- Average annual salary increase: 10 per cent
- Average annual portfolio increase: 4 per cent

We would take another twenty years to hit our net worth target if we lived, saved and invested moderately without taking years off to write, travel or do yoga.

Table 1.1: Twenty-year net worth projection

Rs crore	Y0	Y5	Y10	Y20
Annual income	1.5	2.4	3.9	10.1
Annual savings (20 per cent)	0.3	0.5	0.8	2.0
Total net worth	**0.3**	**2.5**	**6.6**	**25.6**

Source: Created by the author

I was thirty-five years old then. My mind rebelled at the idea of commuting daily to a soulless corporate job until

I was fifty-five years old. Something had to change, but at least now I had a target. I oriented my life around the 4 per cent goal.

Now, your turn to take your first step towards freedom.

Exercise Number 1: What is your liquid net worth target?

- First, calculate the annual expenses of living your desired lifestyle. Consider these ten major categories:
    1. Housing: Rent or housing loan; property taxes; home improvement costs, etc.
    2. Transportation: Car payments or public transport
    3. Food
    4. Utilities
    5. School fees
    6. Insurance
    7. Healthcare
    8. Elderly parent support
    9. Travel and entertainment
    10. Miscellaneous: Clothes, personal care, etc.

- Now, add all these expenses and divide by 4 per cent. You have your net worth target.
- How much time will it take for you to achieve your target if you continue at your current income and expense profile, using industry averages: 10 per cent annual salary increase, 20 per cent annual savings and 4 per cent annual portfolio appreciation net of inflation?

Does the net worth target seem too high and too far away? Don't be intimidated. Aim for the whole world today. The next six rules will get you to your net worth target fast.

'If it's not hard, it's soft'

—Ice Cube

2

Net Impact Rule

My wife and I got to know of her pregnancy the same week I had decided to become a full-time writer in 2015. We reconsidered our decision for what felt like the hundredth time. Who turns full-time writer when they're thirty-six with a kid on the way? Shouldn't we listen to our family's well-meaning advice to 'be practical' after kids? Couldn't I continue to balance my career and writing as I'd already done for a decade since I started writing novels? My head was heavy with doubt. I couldn't shake off the feeling of impending doom in my gut. But I wasn't just trying to become a full-time writer. I was also making my first concentrated effort to increase my net impact. By devoting myself fully to writing, I aimed to write a book that was both interesting enough for millions of people to read and profound enough to impact them deeply. I wouldn't be able to create the same impact as a cog in the corporate wheel. And without increasing my net impact disproportionately, I wouldn't increase my net worth. I had to take the risk at the age of thirty-six, or else I wouldn't be free until the age of fifty-five.

I took the plunge.

Your net worth = Your net impact.

Let's understand what net impact is.

Your net impact = (Magnitude of your impact) x (Depth of your impact)

Impact millions of people with your work (magnitude) and you'll make millions of dollars. Touch people deeply with your creation (depth) and you'll find yourself suddenly, unexpectedly rich. Combine touching millions of people (magnitude) with a deep, profound impact on their lives (depth), and you'll reach your 4 per cent goal faster than the typical retirement paradigm of fifty-five or sixty-five years.

Net Worth = Net Impact

The highest net-worth individuals in the world are people whose products or services touch millions deeply (magnitude x depth), whether through direct ownership, like the founders of Microsoft or Tesla, or through indirect ownership, such as significant investors like Warren Buffett. Similarly, artists like J.K. Rowling and Oprah Winfrey, and sportsmen like Cristiano Ronaldo and Serena Williams, whose actions inspire hope, courage or awe (depth) among millions of people (magnitude) have exceptional net impact and hence, net worth.

In a typical career, you'll impact more people as you go higher in your organization's hierarchy, and hence you hit significant net worth at the top of the corporate ladder, decades after you start your career. A chief executive officer (CEO), for example, earns millions because they have complete authority to create or evolve products and services (depth) touched by millions (magnitude).

How can you reach this apex of impact when you're young versus waiting for your turn in a giant corporate wheel?

The best approach is to build your own product or service that impacts people on a large scale. Another good approach is to join someone who's building something early in their life cycle so that your actions shape the product or service, like early-stage start-up employees do. They shape a start-up as much as the founder does.

MAGNITUDE X DEPTH

Ownership is your key to impact, and hence freedom, at a young age. Without ownership, you'll make a slow, steady ascent to a position of impact, as I did at Procter & Gamble and Kraft, a situation I set out to change in 2015.

My Journey of Ownership and Failure

I wrote *The Seeker*, my third novel, through 2013 and '14, finally turning into a full-time writer in 2015 at the age of thirty-six. With my first single-minded effort at writing, I wrote a novel that was both a page-turning thriller (magnitude: millions read thrillers) and inspired people to pursue their deepest spiritual calling (depth).

Or so I thought.

Over 2013 and '14, I was rejected by sixty-one literary agents one after the other after submitting my manuscript.

I'd ask for feedback from everyone who rejected the book. A few literary agents were kind enough to share what wasn't working. The protagonist's quest wasn't relatable, the plot was too slow in the beginning, the secondary characters were flat. With each feedback, I improved the book. This time, I wanted to write the perfect book that would be published by a top US publishing house globally so that millions around the world read it, not just a subsection of Indian readers who'd read my previous novels, *Keep Off the Grass* and *Johnny Gone Down*, which were published only in India.

I was able to concentrate more after becoming a full-time writer. I read more than sixty books about the Bronx housing projects where my protagonist grew up in the 1970s, just to write the first page well, where he reveals his motivations for his quest. Beta readers told me that the plot came to life only after the protagonist moved from New York to the Indian Himalayas, so I cut the first fifty pages of the book. I restructured the book to get the protagonist to India faster, where he enters a secret world with hidden yoga ashrams and holy men with miraculous powers. I also added more depth to each of the secondary characters' journeys so that all characters in the book were empathetic and relatable.

I kept revising the book daily for another nine months. During this period, I read many more books on writing to improve my understanding of developing plots and characters, took multiple writing courses with Gotham, the New York fiction-writing school, and spent every lunch break researching articles on the Internet on tips to improve my writing. I'd often despair after the rejections. My wife was pregnant with our second daughter in 2015. With no formal employment, we were paying for health insurance out of our own pockets. I'd given myself eighteen months to make it as a full-time writer, based on our savings, and time was dwindling fast. I kept myself calm with my daily meditation practice, even though it seemed as if the world was crashing around me. Rejections just meant that I had to work harder on my characters and plot (depth) so that I could inspire millions with the book (magnitude).

The Seeker was finally accepted by Penguin Random House US and was published worldwide under the title *The Yoga of Max's Discontent* in May 2016.

The novel failed almost immediately after launch. Penguin Random House sold 25,000 copies, less than half the sales of my previous novels, both of which had sold more than 50,000 copies each, although this was a worldwide release while the other novels had released only in India. Three months into the launch, the publisher informed me that they would turn the excess, unsold copies into pulp, a major humiliation for a writer. I was numb that day. I was not only disappointed with the disastrous audience response after three years of 24x7 obsession, but also worried about my future. With my dwindling savings, I would have to go back to a corporate career, but I continued to feel discomfited with consumer-packaged goods. What would I do next?

First, however, I had to evaluate my failure ruthlessly. The novel had over 200 five-star reviews on Amazon

US and was appreciated by literary critics in esteemed publications like *Publishers Weekly* and *The New York Review of Books*; so I had succeeded in depth. But I had failed in magnitude. People hadn't related to the core theme of spiritual enlightenment. No one was talking about the book or telling their friends to read it. I could try to write a more compelling plot next, with stronger characters, but creativity would always be subjective. Was there a more objective way to use my writing expertise to have an impact on a large scale?

In my quest for financial freedom, I'd been reading a lot about online passive income and 'four-hour work weeks'. The theory was appealing on paper. You created a unique product, physical or digital, for which people were searching the Internet, and made them aware of it by placing digital advertising right next to the search term. People would click on the link and buy the product. All you had to do was to put a one-time effort into creating the product. Then, it would sell by itself daily, predictably, as new users searched for it every day. I was intrigued by the prospect of creating online courses in my expertise areas, starting with writing and publishing, and dived full-force into designing and launching one.

The Failed Passive-Income Experiment

Surveys indicate that more than 80 per cent of people want to write a book[1] but there are no structured online courses for the whole journey, from writing to publishing, for laypeople. I had just been through the entire process, so I created a detailed online video course on how to write a book that gets published by a top publishing house. The course had information no writer had shared before—exact writing structures, the verbatim query letter which had got me a literary agent, and the names and contacts of the sixty top literary agents in the US who responded to cold queries. Early feedback from my corporate and writer friends was positive. They got confidence from the course material to turn ideas they had been playing with in their minds for years into books. They'd pay for it.

I launched the course with much expectation. After the success of the writing course, I planned to do courses on business, meditation and other passion areas to keep earning passive income to support our family while writing my next novel.

I spent three months hustling before I realized that passive income online is a myth.

Again, it fails the net impact principle.

You may create a great online course (depth), but the task of getting users (magnitude) means there's nothing passive about it. Instead of writing a novel on the side, my time quickly filled up with getting more folks to sign up for the course with guest blogs, paid advertising, partnerships and barter deals.

The work was 24x7 active.

The only people making passive income online are the ones selling courses on how to make passive income online to unsuspecting people; and I suspect even that's not fully passive as I see them hustling all the time with new funnels, new podcasts, etc.

I gave up on this solo entrepreneurship experience in three months. I'd planned to do online courses as a side income while I wrote my next novel with magnitude and depth. If I had to be active 24x7 to make money, I wanted to create something that mattered on a much larger scale in the world.

My next ownership venture had to impact millions (magnitude) and truly touch the depth of the human spirit (depth).

But first, I had to solve the problem of my shrinking bank balance. I had nothing to show for eighteen months of full-time writing. With two kids under two, I was out of time for new experiments.

WhiteHat Jr: Magnitude and Depth

With a sinking feeling in my gut, I updated my résumé and reached out to headhunters and ex-colleagues for jobs in July 2016. My heart wasn't in corporate life any more. But I had taken my chance at independence and couldn't make it work. Now, I had to give it all to my job search.

I was surprised by how receptive the corporate world was to my re-entry, given my previous difficult post-sabbatical experiences. Tech start-ups had normalized, even glorified, failure. A few human resources managers frowned at my discontinuous résumé with long gaps for travel and writing, but most hiring managers seemed to appreciate my constant thrust to grow. I'd been promoted fast in my career at both Procter & Gamble and Kraft, from assistant brand manager to brand manager to director, then senior director and head of marketing, and knew brand management fundamentals well. Plus, the hands-on digital experience I'd gained by spending my own money to market my novels on Facebook and Google and create fully automated digital funnels for an online course was an asset for legacy companies in the new world.

I'd been tense about finding a job after an eighteen-month career gap, but within two months of searching, I had a job offer for a marketing head role for a major consumer-packaged goods brand in Vermont, a lucrative central marketing role for a private equity firm in Connecticut, the head of marketing role for Uber in India, and multiple other roles in the pipeline. I was pulled to only one role, however. Discovery Communications had been searching for almost a year for a leader in India who could combine business acumen with creative passion to shake up their television channels' business in India. My fifteen years in consumer products, combined with my fiction-writing career, seemed to fit the bill perfectly.

In turn, my heart lifted at the idea of running a purpose-driven organization like Discovery. I'd also experienced Discovery's mission in a very personal way. During our 2013 sabbatical, my wife and I were doing a day hike in the Himalayas when there was sudden, heavy snowfall in late afternoon. We were stranded on the way to Gaumukh, the headstream of the Ganga, with just our thin sleeping bags in a bare wooden shelter. With little food and only two warm layers, we had to make our way down as soon as we could to prevent hypothermia. We started off at dawn the next day and had walked barely a kilometre in the 11-kilometre hike down when the snow started to melt, forming a thin layer of water on its surface. Our shoes slipped in the melting ice. The Gangotri National Park had opened just a day before for hiking in early April, so there were no overnight hikers or guides around for help. One false step and we would hurtle down to certain death thousands of feet into the valley below. We were stuck, unable to decide whether to hike down and risk death by slipping in the melting ice or move up, where we'd risk life again, given the freezing cold and no food supplies. For the first time in our years of hiking, we worried about losing our lives.

In a flash, however, I remembered an episode from *Man vs Wild with Bear Grylls* where Bear had put his socks over his shoes to prevent himself from slipping in the fresh ice. We followed suit. It worked. With the friction from the socks, our shoes held on the slippery ice. We made our way down, hanging on for dear life on the sides of the fresh snow. Discovery had saved my life.

As a result, I believed in Discovery's mission of inspiring curiosity by opening windows to new worlds very personally. All my worries about re-entering the consumer culture dissipated. We moved from the US to India, and I threw myself fully into the role.

Discovery had launched in India twenty years back in 1995, but had less than 1 per cent share of the Indian media market, a fraction of their strength in Europe and the US. India consumed 95 per cent of its media content in Hindi and regional languages, and Discovery hadn't been able to penetrate the mass market fully with its international content. Hence, I focused single-mindedly on creating more local content for Discovery to take their mission to the last mile in India. We took big leaps. Some projects worked—for instance, the Discovery Kids channel rose to the top three after being the last in the genre since its launch more than five years ago. Other big bets, like the Hindi purpose-driven general entertainment channel, Discovery Jeet, failed. I considered Discovery my own company and the business failures hurt as much as personal failures. So I learnt from them, but never stopped pitching new ideas to the Discovery US headquarters to expand their presence in India. The Discovery global team took notice of the sudden energy in their India operation after years of stagnancy. They asked me to lead Discovery's content team in Asia. I considered the role, but I couldn't ignore the sinking feeling in my gut that I'd settled in my comfort zone.

I was almost three years into the job, one of the youngest country heads in corporate India and high in demand for international organizations looking to turn around their stagnant growth in India with bold moves. My career would perhaps continue to do well. Our children, who'd been six months and two years old when we moved, had settled well in Mumbai. I was taking big bets in Discovery but always had the comfortable corporate cushion to fall back upon.

Yes, it was an entrepreneurial job. But it was still a job. I still worked for a boss. I was no closer to the vision of independence I'd set five years ago. Should I let go of the dream? Isn't this as good as it gets?

I've often found answers to my biggest questions in life in storytelling constructs. We're all living our stories, and what works for a good story typically works for a good life. What makes a good story? I had found the LOCK format useful for my novels:[2]

L: Lead
O: Objective
C: Conflict
K: Knockout

Take any iconic story, for example, *The Shawshank Redemption* or *The Godfather*. They follow the same construct. You have a lead character (L: lead), who has a big, selfless objective (O: objective), and faces tremendous conflict in his path to accomplish this objective (C: conflict). Eventually the lead character either achieves his goal or he doesn't (K: knockout). But he is still a hero for having attempted to achieve such a big, selfless goal. The protagonist in *The Shawshank Redemption* wanted justice, the Godfather fought for his family's honour, Superman wanted to save the world, the heroes in *3 Idiots* wanted to change the Indian education system; the bigger and more selfless the objective, the bigger will be the conflict, and hence the bigger the story. Whether they win or lose is almost secondary to their transformation. We admire these characters because of the audacity of their goals, and we're inspired by their stories because they face the life-or-death conflicts inherent in pursuing big goals with relentless determination.

Just like life.

The bigger and more selfless the leads' goal, the bigger will be their story. Whether they're trying to put man on Mars like Elon Musk or eliminate malaria from the world like Bill Gates, the most compelling characters of our generation are the ones with the biggest, most selfless goals, who go all out to achieve them.

My own story was becoming smaller. A decade later, I would be a minor footnote in Discovery's global history. What was the big, selfless goal I was pursuing? How was I transforming if I wasn't overcoming a do-or-die conflict daily? I had to search for a goal with magnitude and depth once again.

In my excitement at leading Discovery India, I'd read books, blogs and articles on technology throughout my tenure to understand how I could make Discovery more technology-centric than a typical legacy media company. Now, I used the knowledge to brainstorm my own technology start-up ideas. I considered applying artificial intelligence models to Indian gene data to create predictive healthcare plans for a large mass of Indian people who couldn't afford regular medical testing. Another start-up idea I evaluated was giving urban consumers direct access to rural farmers' produce by eliminating supply-chain inefficiencies. But I was most drawn to the WhiteHat Jr idea, that of making kids creators versus consumers of technology.

My children, then four and two years old, were just entering the mainstream school system. Despite the technological revolution sweeping the world, my kids' school curriculum was not meaningfully different from the one we had when I'd graduated more than twenty years ago. Creation would be the foundation of meaningful careers in a future where every routine job would be automated, and yet, school pedagogy still emphasized rote learning. Studies[3] have shown that while 98 per cent of five-year-old kids are imaginative or creative, only 2 per cent of adults can be considered creative. Children become less and less creative as more and more binary- and rule-based thinking enters their life.

Also, one of my biggest regrets was that I had started building things too late. I'd never been encouraged to pursue writing or any creative hobby in school or at home. In 2007,

I wrote my first novel at the age of twenty-five because I was lonely and needed something to fill my days. Little did I know that the first act of creation would transform my life.

From riding across India in a motorcycle to learning Vipassana meditation in a ten-day silent retreat at Dharamshala in the Himalayas, I'd poured all the life experiences that had shaped me in *Keep Off the Grass*, my first novel. I attempted a second novel in early 2008 and realized I was repeating the same ideas and experiences again. Instead of writing more, I left my job to travel in 2008. Without the first act of creation and the empty creative well after, I would've perhaps not sought more travel and life experiences. I felt the same creative vacuum after *Johnny Gone Down*, my second novel, was published in 2010. Everything I'd learnt about a boundary-less world from backpacking was captured in the novel. I had nothing more to say, so I sought more experiences to write my third novel, *The Seeker.* Creation led to growth, growth led to more creation; it was a virtuous cycle I wanted every kid to experience, so that they lived a life of meaning forever.

Hence I started WhiteHat Jr with the vision for kids to create remarkable things in the world with technology, and identify themselves as creators for life.

WhiteHat Jr's mission, therefore, had both magnitude—every kid in the world deserves to be a builder—and depth—finding life's highest meaning by creating versus consuming is a deep, fundamental human yearning.

The Difficulty of Doing Good

Why did WhiteHat Jr work when *The Seeker* didn't?

On paper, both ideas had magnitude and depth. In real life, they received an equally cold response when I pitched them. *The Seeker* was rejected sixty-one times. In WhiteHat Jr's case, the CEO of a major Indian technology company, who was my acquaintance, said that the idea was too small and would never work, when I told him the day after I came up with it. Another friend in technology told me it was too ahead of its time. Everyone to whom I pitched it in the first month said that I was committing career suicide by leaving the role of the head of Discovery India to pursue WhiteHat Jr.

Then, the ideas found believers. *The Seeker* found Penguin Random House, who published it worldwide. WhiteHat Jr found early backers in Nexus Venture Partners and Omidyar Networks, the venture capitalist firms who invested Rs 10 crore ($1.3 million) in seed funding when I'd created just a bare prototype of the product.

Both the novel and the company were executed with the same passion and precision.

Yet one worked and the other didn't.

Net impact ideas always lie at the edges of the system, never at the centre of it. They meet a deep, unarticulated human yearning. If users had clearly articulated the need, any established system could meet it. No one would need a new company for it. Given that the ideas they're pursuing are so off the centre, both start-ups and novels, like all creation industries, have a 10 per cent success rate.[4] For every Harry Potter or Facebook, which successfully enters the mainstream, there'll be nine other ideas that remain on the edges. No one can truly predict which ideas will go from the edges to the centre. You just need to show up daily and keep trying.

An average successful start-up takes seven years from initiation to exit.[5] An average novelist has written five rejected novels before publication.[6] My own start-up tenure was short, from 2018 to 2020, but the journey of pursuing magnitude and depth started seven years ago in 2013 when I first plunged full-time into writing.

What is your net impact idea?

You'll also perhaps spend seven years obsessively trying to make it work. Everyone will dismiss your irrational belief in your idea. Like me, you may fail in the first and second tries. But don't let that discourage you. Keep pursuing ideas of great magnitude and depth one after the other, and one day you'll bring one idea from the edge to the centre. Then, your net worth will match your net impact.

Now, it's your turn.

Exercise Number 2: What is the One Net Impact Idea You're Deeply Obsessed With?

- Does it touch millions of people (magnitude)?
- Does it meet a deep, fundamental human need (depth)?

Be ruthless with your evaluation. But don't be discouraged if your idea doesn't meet the magnitude and depth criteria. Do this next:

1. Brainstorm three alternatives to your idea. Does any of them pass the magnitude and depth test?

2. List down the people you know or have heard of who're creating something with depth and magnitude. Can you join them? The first fifty key hires of WhiteHat Jr were like co-owners of the company, shaping the company through their vision, and they earned the same meaningful rewards from their equity ownership as I did.
3. Don't be discouraged if neither of the above works for you. Research daily how technology is changing your industry and what ideas new Indian, Chinese and US unicorns are pursuing. Keep writing down ideas by which you get inspired to find THE ONE ownership idea for which you'll put everything on the line.

'Take up one idea. Make that one idea your life—think of it, dream of it, live on that idea. Let the brain, muscles, nerves, every part of your body, be full of that idea, and just leave every other idea alone. This is the way to success.'

—Swami Vivekananda

3

Salary/14 Lakh Quitting Rule

THREE months after I started WhiteHat Jr in 2018, my ex-colleague from Discovery came to visit me at our 'first office' late in the evening one day. We were seven people working in the living room of my house in Mumbai. We'd just launched our first version of the product—kids built an app of their choice with a teacher, over eight live classes on an open-source video platform. We'd shared the details about the course on our personal Facebook pages, and I was calling the first 250 users who'd completed a free trial class one by one.

Each call was similar. Kids loved the creative activity in the class and the warmth of a live teacher, but parents were confused. What was coding? How do live classes work? Will this help with school grades? I'd explain to parents the research on how coding made kids creators for life[1] and why having the confidence to build things from scratch was the single most important skill that would matter in the new world. I made seventy calls that day. Most parents put the phone down in the middle of the conversation. Others asked me to call back in an hour and never picked up the call. Only a few expressed interest to know more about the classes. In the middle of these calls and making diligent follow-up notes on Google Sheets on whom to call back, I would fix the computer audio and video settings for new people joining our trial classes, since I was also our very first call-centre employee.

My ex-colleague from Discovery looked at the frenzied activity in our living room with puzzlement.

He had the same unasked question in his eyes that I'd seen in the eyes of friends and ex-colleagues who'd visited me in the early days of WhiteHat Jr.

Why would anyone in their right mind leave the role of the head of Discovery India to do a dead-end job like this one?

'This is going to take a while to work, isn't it?' he finally said aloud, without much hope. 'How long will your savings last?'

I didn't have a convincing answer for that unasked question, except that I was following an instinct of magnitude and depth with full energy once again. For his question spoken aloud, however, I had a mathematical answer: twenty-two months.

I would give it my all for twenty-two months. Then, I'd look for a job again. Until then, I'd keep diluting my savings to fund WhiteHat Jr.

How Long Will Your Savings Last? Salary/14 Lakh Quitting Rule

Can you quit your job to pursue your net impact idea? Use the salary/14 lakh quitting rule to answer your question objectively.

(Your annual salary)/(Rs 14 lakh) is the number of months you need to find a job if your net impact plunge doesn't work out.

First, calculate your total liquid savings—cash, equity, bonds, fixed deposits, anything that can be converted into cash easily, not fixed assets such as houses, land or cars, unless you're ready to convert them to cash immediately. Now, divide this with your all-in monthly expenses, including your household expenses and the cash you need to fund your idea, if any. From this, subtract the number of months you'll need to look for a job if your venture doesn't succeed, using the salary/14 lakh quitting rule.

The number of months your savings will last for you to pursue your net impact idea uninhibitedly = (Liquid savings/Monthly expenses) – (Salary/14 lakh).

For example, if you have Rs 80 lakh of liquid savings in cash and stock, and Rs 5 lakh as all-in monthly expenses, your savings will last 80/5 i.e., sixteen months.

Now, you don't want to be out of money when you're looking for a job. That's where the salary/14 lakh rule comes in. If your salary was Rs 42 lakh per year, then it would take (42 lakh/14 lakh), i.e., three months to find a job.

So, deducting this from the earlier calculated sixteen, you get thirteen full months, which is the time you have to uninhibitedly pursue your idea without fear or regret. Then, pivot completely to look for a job.

If you want to be more conservative, as I became once we had children, you can use the worst-case scenario of salary/7 lakh rule to find a job.

SALARY/14 RULE

In the example above, change your time to find a job to (Rs 42 lakh/7 lakh), i.e., six months. So now, you have (16–6), i.e., ten months to pursue your idea.

I started WhiteHat Jr with my own savings in July 2018. With no co-founder, I covered the founding team's salary, office infrastructure and IT server and membership costs for four months. We were spending Rs 10 lakh per month. Without the rule, I would have panicked at my savings depleting rapidly but with the rule, I knew I had twenty-two months to make a go for it. I was still tense every day, micromanaging each expense, from buying the lowest-quality bean bags to not shifting the office from our living room until the neighbours complained about the throngs of chattering, excited kids, who were testing the first version of our product, coming in and out of our house. But the rule gave me the comfort to dig in and keep making the product in the face of venture capitalist (VC) rejections.

I'd reached out to each of the top thirty VCs in India immediately after our prototype was done. We were rejected by twenty of them within a week without their meeting the team or hearing our presentation, since they didn't think the market was big enough. Most of these twenty rejections were quick after one phone call, but once a top VC from Bengaluru made me wait for seven hours in her office reception area before rejecting my idea within a few minutes of meeting. You learn to accept the idiosyncrasies of VCs in the pitching process. We kept pitching enthusiastically to the remaining ten, going through the lengthy process followed by all top venture capitalists.

First, one had to present one's case to a junior analyst. The analyst built conviction by interviewing one's employees and customers and running detailed analyses on one's business model. Then, one met the partner, who developed the same conviction after repeating a shorter version of the same process. If one made it this far, one made a presentation to the Investment Committee (IC) members. After more follow-up analyses on the business model and team, they decided whether to fund the company or not. Once they green lit the investment, legal and audit teams of the VC would audit the company structure and financials. Finally, the money would be wired to one's company's bank account. The end-to-end process from initiating contact with a VC to the funding being deposited in one's bank account could take from three to six months for an early-stage start-up like ours.

Seven of the remaining ten VCs rejected us at various stages in this process. I continued to invest in the team and the product during this period. A functioning product in the IC meetings helped us get term sheets from the remaining three VCs, out of which I went with Nexus Venture Partners and Omidyar Networks. We got a seed investment to get the company started.

Despite funding, I took a 90 per cent salary cut from my salary as the country head in Discovery, given the small scale of our venture. Now, I was funding the company with investor funding but still diluting my personal savings to cover our household expenses. Again, the salary/14 lakh rule kept me calm enough to not make any drastic and distracting changes like shifting our home to a cheaper location or downgrading our kids' schools. Each month, I would sell off our stocks to meet our household expenses for the month. I was making an investment in increasing my net impact. My savings were a small trade-off for that.

Salary/14 Lakh Rule Rationale

A study by First Transitions in 2005, of 435 US job seekers, indicates that (salary)/$20,000 is the number of months it takes to find a job in the US.[2]

For example, one may find an entry-level job as a retail-store employee quickly, since many such jobs are available. However, as one moves up the hierarchy—say, becomes a highly-paid CEO—one would take longer to find a job since fewer comparable jobs are available at the top of the pyramid.

The top 10 per cent of Indian households with incomes >$25,000, the members of which are most likely to leave their corporate jobs to take a full-time ownership plunge, have a similar supply–demand job equation as a white-collar American. Hence, I had a starting hypothesis of converting $20,000 directly to Indian rupees as Rs 14 lakh.

Next, given the stakes of what I'm recommending here for my readers, I commissioned a large-scale study with RedCore, India's premier primary research agency, to identify the exact time it takes to find a job in India after a career break. The results were surprisingly conclusive. You need *sixty days* to find a job after a career break in India. The two-month rule remains consistent across income groups.

Table 3.1: Time taken to find a job after a career break (Average length of career break = Ten months)

RedCore sample size (Number of survey respondents with career breaks)	Annual income	Average time taken to find a job after career break (months)
46	< Rs 10 lakh	2
45	Rs 10–25 lakh	2.1
40	Rs 25–50 lakh	2.2
33	>Rs 50 lakh	2.1

Source: RedCore Primary Research: Job Switching Dynamics, May 2022

Further, 85 per cent of the people who took a career break actually reported a salary *increase* on returning to the workforce, indicating the normalization of growth-oriented career breaks in white-collar India.

Table 3.2: Compensation shifts after a career break

Compensation shift after career break	**Percentage of respondents (N=164)**
Compensation less than or equal to previous job	**15**
0–10% Increase	**13**
11–20% Increase	**28**
>20% Increase	**44**

Source: RedCore Primary Research: Job Switching Dynamics, May 2022

People took a career break for multiple reasons, from travelling and recharging (45 per cent) to studying (27 per cent), entrepreneurial stints (6 per cent) and maternity and other reasons (22 per cent). In most cases, as Table 3.2 shows, the world rewarded them for their growth instead of penalizing them.

You can therefore be assured that the salary/14 lakh or the 60-day rule, whichever is higher in your case, is a very sensible, research-based benchmark to use for your job search. For the more risk-averse, use salary/7 lakh as a conservative metric to account for global financial crises and other black-swan events.

Psychological Preparation for the Salary/14 Lakh Rule

How do you prepare yourself psychologically to see your savings deplete month after month while you pursue your net impact idea, even if you know the rule works?

I'd first used the salary/14 lakh rule in 2015 to calculate that I had eighteen months to make it as a full-time writer before looking for a job. For this eighteen-month period, I planned to live life as usual. My wife got pregnant with our second daughter. Our friends and family asked me often what my broader plan was. I was among the top rankers at my engineering college and IIM. How could I have become so irresponsible as to live in New York City with no job but with young kids at age thirty-five? No one understood my complex calculations. Every so often, people's doubts would rub off on me and I'd make drastic plans to cut our expenses. We contemplated moving from New York to Cuenca, an artistic but cheap expat city in

Ecuador, South America, and even visited there to look at rental apartments. I would consider taking up a marketing consulting project for companies in my network to make a side income. In my lowest moments, I thought of restricting my full-time writing period to six months only. What stopped me from taking drastic decisions was an exercise from Stoic philosophy called fear-setting that I learnt from the author Tim Ferriss.[3]

I would ask myself three fear-based questions in moments of self-doubt:

1. What is the absolute worst that can happen if I continue down this path?
2. What action shall I take to resolve that worst-case scenario?
3. Reverse fear: What will happen if I stop walking down this path?

Then, I would write specific, honest answers to each of them. For example, during my full-time writing period, I wrote the following:

1. My worst-case scenario is that the salary/14 lakh rule doesn't work and I can't find a job, especially if the economy goes through an unexpected downturn. Our family will be in extreme mental stress as we'll run out of our savings just as our kids are about to enter the expensive New York school system.
2. I've taken the action of planning for the worst case by having enough savings to cover the worst-case salary/7 lakh scenario of looking for a job. If even that proves

insufficient, I shall take a salary cut and take up the job of brand manager in a small company, as many would be happy to have a former director from Procter & Gamble and Kraft join them in a junior role. We shall move to a small city and live comfortably on the salary since it's still much higher than the US median salary. I would regret that my career was set back by a decade but I would consider this regret a minor cost for a major attempt at living my dream life.

3. On the other hand, if I don't continue down the full-time writing path and give up early in fear, I shall always regret not taking my chance at increasing my net impact. Twenty years later, I won't respect myself for having folded so early when I wanted to break the 'freedom-at-fifty-five' paradigm for good.

This exercise was magical for me. My apprehensions would go away almost immediately after writing down my answers. Naming your worst fear dissipates the vague sense of uneasiness you inevitably feel when you walk down unconventional paths. Then, creating specific action plans gives you the confidence that you have the agency to solve all problems that come your way. Finally, you realize that the risk of action is almost always better than the regret of inaction.

I would refocus on my fiction writing after doing this exercise, rather than distract myself by moving countries or shifting from a full-time job to a consulting job. Eighteen months later, when my writing didn't yield results, none of my worst-case scenarios materialized. I found the job as head of Discovery almost immediately.

I repeated the same exercise when I left Discovery to start WhiteHat Jr. First, I named my fear of never finding such a prestigious and impact-oriented job as a country head ever again. Then, I embraced the action plan of finding a role a few notches below the role of a country head in another purpose-driven company and working up my way again. Finally, I reminded myself of the reverse fear—the regret I'd feel a decade later for having missed the chance to build a tech product with my hands in my forties, perhaps the last time I would be able to do this in my life. I took the plunge. Once again, the worst-case scenario didn't happen.

Over multiple acts of leaving my job to pursue travel, yoga, writing and then a start-up, I've concluded that extraordinary growth events hurt massively in the short term but always pay back in the long term. I'd lived my worst-case scenario, for example, on return from my first backpacking sabbatical in 2008 when I was sleeping on my sister's couch. In the short term, I had nothing to show in terms of my growth as a writer and a professional from a more boundary-less view of the world. In the long term, however, my travels seeped into every part of my life. I'd gone backpacking across South America, using hand gestures to cross the Amazon by boat from Manaus in Brazil to Iquitos in Peru. Even in the deepest belly of countries where I didn't speak a word of the language, I'd been able to get by easily with the language of the heart. As a result, I had complete confidence to launch early versions of WhiteHat Jr in the US, the UK, Australia, Brazil and Mexico instead of waiting to perfect the product in India over many years, as most Indian companies do before expanding. People are more similar than dissimilar throughout the world, and a product that meets a deep human yearning would work well globally. WhiteHat Jr grew rapidly from this early international expansion.

Similarly, *The Seeker* didn't work but I wouldn't have got the role of the head of Discovery at a young age without the creative depth I gained from this novel. The world's systems are inefficient in the short term but efficient in the long term. If you grow ten times when you throw yourself into gaining mastery in a new field instead of growing one time by ticking boxes in your current job, the world eventually rewards you for the tenfold growth. Your extraordinary internal growth will eventually always lead to discontinuous external growth.

Does the salary/14 lakh rule allow you to pursue your net impact idea full-time?

Plunge into it and make the idea your life.

You'll trade personal savings for growth. But over-saving can often be a bigger problem than overspending. Choose large life experiences over large bank balances. Long-term personal growth and financial growth have an almost perfect correlation.

Now, it's your turn.

Exercise Number 3: Can You Quit Your Job to Pursue Your Net-Impact Idea?

1. Calculate

- What is your total liquid savings—cash, stock, bonds, fixed deposits?

- What are your all-in monthly expenses, both living expenses and your costs of funding your net-impact idea each month?
- What is your current monthly salary?

2. Analyse

- Likely scenario of number of months to pursue your idea = Liquid savings/Monthly expenses – Salary/14 lakh or RedCore 60-Day Rule (whichever is higher).
- Worst-case scenario number of months to pursue your idea = Liquid savings/Monthly expenses – Salary/7 lakh

3. Plunge

- Write down your biggest fear of taking the plunge.
- Create a specific action plan to mitigate the scenario above.
- Write down what will happen if you don't take the plunge.

Now, go with your instinct.

'Forget safety. Live where you fear to live. Destroy your reputation. Be notorious. I have tried prudent planning long enough. From now on I'll be mad.'

—Rumi

4

'30x7' Ownership Shift

Nine months into WhiteHat Jr in March 2019, we were conducting 500 live coding classes per day. Our thirty-member team was all hands on deck. My phone was set sixth on the roster as backup to our five-member in-house call-centre team. Our classes and call volumes would peak on Saturday and Sunday mornings at 9 a.m. when the maximum number of kids joined the classes on their days off from school. My official work timings were 10x10x6, that is, 10a.m.–10p.m., six days a week, Monday–Saturday; so I'd be with my daughters in the playground on Sunday when my phone would start ringing non-stop. I'd guide customers to fix a range of issues, from changing their Windows system microphone settings, so that both teachers and students could hear each other, to updating the Google Chrome browser for cameras to work without incident, while pushing my daughters higher on the playground swings. I fervently wished for our Series A funding round to close quickly so that we could outsource our call centre, and our team could spend undistracted time with their families for at least a few hours on Saturdays and Sundays.

We closed our Series A six months later in October 2019. Alas, peace remained elusive! We launched in the US at the same time when we were increasing our presence in India. Now, mornings were spent on India's scaling concerns and late nights on the teething issues in the US. One day, our founding team stayed in the office fifty hours at a stretch as we covered both day and night shifts to speak to customers and get to the heart of how we would differentiate the curriculum between India and the US.

Ownership consumes you.

I was compressing thirty years of regular corporate experience in the seven years I pursued ownership projects, from starting writing my novel full-time in 2014 to leaving WhiteHat Jr in 2021.

I wish I'd done it sooner.

30X7

Ownership compresses thirty years of low-intensity corporate work into seven years of high-intensity work, and rewards you proportionately in terms of personal, professional and financial growth.

A successful start-up in India takes about seven years from initiation to exit. The best corporate careers will take thirty years, from joining at an entry-level position to becoming a CEO.[1]

Embrace the 30x7 obsessive work ethic as an owner.

A regular job gives you average work–life balance for thirty years or more.

Now as an owner, accept *temporary work–life imbalance* for seven years for a lifetime of freedom later.

Your 30x7 Preparation: Learn, Reflect, Execute

Four weeks of yoga teacher's training prepared me more for handling a start-up than two decades of my corporate career. I'd done only four one-hour classes of yoga in New York before our 2013 sabbatical, when my wife and I decided to do a full-time yoga teacher's training at Sivananda Ashram in Madurai, Tamil Nadu. The ashram typically didn't have rank beginners like me signing up for a teacher's training course, but I was fortunate that they had structured the course assuming people would have limited exposure to traditional yoga, even if they practised modern yoga styles. In a four-week syllabus, the course compressed knowledge across a range of fields, from yoga's spiritual roots to the theory of yoga's anatomical impact and the actual physical practice of all critical yoga asanas. I was intimidated by the schedule. We had to go non-stop for six days a week, from 5.20 a.m., when we were woken up by a gong in the shared dormitory where I lived with sixty other attendees, to lights off at 10.30 p.m. (see Table 4.1).

Table 4.1: Yoga teacher's training course schedule

5.20 a.m.	Wake up
6–7.30 a.m.	Satsang (group meditation, chanting and discourse)
7.30–8 a.m.	Tea break
8–10 a.m.	Yoga asana (physical practice)
10–11a.m.	Lunch
11–12.30 p.m.	Karmayoga (assigned duties varied from sweeping ashram floors and cleaning bathrooms to washing dishes)
12.30–1.30 p.m.	Asana coaching
1.30–2 p.m.	Tea break
2–3.30 p.m.	The Bhagavadgita or Vedanta philosophy lecture
3.30–6 p.m.	Yoga asana (physical practice)
6–8 p.m.	Dinner
8–10.30 p.m.	Satsang (group meditation, chanting and discourse)
10.30 p.m.	Lights off

Source: Created by the author

Attendance was compulsory for each session. You got called to the ashram administration office if you missed a class. Each missed class had to be explained with a written submission and more than three missed classes meant expulsion from the course. The ashram was also very disciplined about uniforms, and the time between sessions was spent in changing from the yellow-hued holy clothes to the more stretchable physical asana uniform and back for the theory classes. We had to complete a written summary of what we had learnt in the theory class daily, and each week, we had to demonstrate our mastery of the physical yoga asanas by performing them correctly in front of the course instructor. At the end of the course, one had to appear for a detailed four-hour-long written examination in which one needed a passing grade to complete one's certification. My mind rebelled at the draconian schedule. I'd count the days left for the course to end and hold my breath to stop blaming my wife who was an avid yoga practitioner and had advocated doing the structured teacher's training course versus just living in an ashram as I'd suggested. Our sabbatical clock was ticking, and I had had no time to think and travel, which I'd assumed would be as crucial and insightful as yoga was. I wanted to leave midway.

I was wrong. I'm glad I stayed. The Sivananda yoga teacher's training was among the most insightful learning experiences of my life. By the end of the four weeks, I went from not being able to touch my toes to standing on my head, and from having a superficial understanding of yoga to a profound appreciation of the physical, mental and spiritual benefits of the practice.

Figure 4.1: Vedantic learning framework

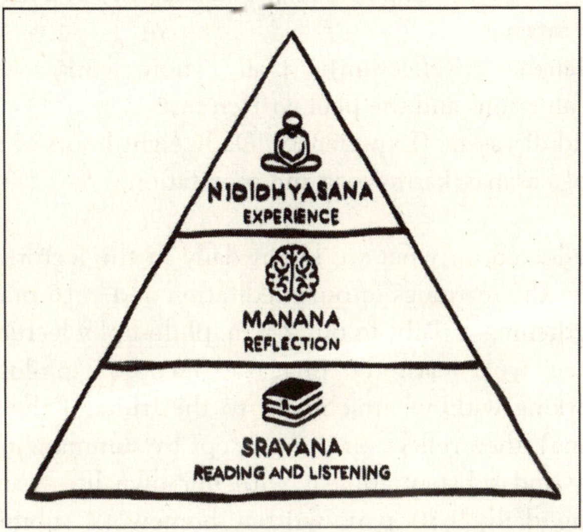

Source: Created by the author

Unknown to me, the course was following an ancient Vedanta learning framework for helping someone gain mastery over a topic. First, you read and listened to all secondary knowledge about the subject (sravana); then, you reflected and formed your own thesis about the subject (manana); and finally, you made the subject a living, breathing reality by experiencing it directly (nidhidhyasana). Only reading and reflecting would not lead to mastery, and jumping impatiently into experience would mean reinventing the wheel and repeating the same mistakes made by millions before you.

Sivananda Ashram had followed the exact framework in the course:

- Sravana (Reading/Listening): Daily three hours of lectures on yoga philosophy and anatomy and listening to satsang.
- Manana (Reflection): Daily homework, weekly evaluations and the final written test.
- Nididhyasana (Experience): Daily eight hours of hatha yoga asanas, karmayoga and meditation.

We reflected on what we learnt daily in the lectures and applied the learnings in our meditation and yoga practice, strengthening it daily. In our 2 p.m. philosophy lecture, for instance, we'd learn the Bhagavadgita's core philosophy of working without attachment to the fruits of the work (sravana), then reflect on the concept by summarizing the theory and substantiating it with our own life examples for the daily 9.30 p.m. written homework submission (manana), and incorporate the philosophy in living next day at noon by wiping the floors of our large, open-air dormitory without grudging the storm that had littered tree branches and dirt all over the room (nididhyasana). The yoga concepts became a living, breathing reality with this practice.

On return from our sabbatical in 2013, I followed this exact Vedanta learning framework to gain mastery over new fields in compressed periods. I'd written novels before but I relearnt writing when I became a full-time writer by reading sixty or seventy books on writing over three months, and continuing learning how to be a better writer by reading blogs and articles daily during my lunch break (sravana). Then I outlined my novel in detail over two weeks. I used the LOCK method—lead, objective, conflict, knockout—for the overall plot as well as each of the primary characters' journeys. I also wrote detailed physical descriptions and emotional back stories of the characters as well as the specific ways the book's setting in the Indian Himalayas would impact the characters (manana). Finally, I wrote the book with discipline daily for six months, spending a minimum of eight hours from 9 a.m. to 7 p.m., with a one-hour break each for yoga and lunch, and continuing post-dinner if I hadn't completed my goal of 1,500 words per day (nididhyasana).

Later in 2016, I used the same learning framework to understand media in a short time when I was heading Discovery. Then, for the very first version of WhiteHat Jr in 2018, I read more than seventy start-up and technology books, and a select list of blogs and podcast transcripts over three months (sravana); sketched in twenty-five charts the exact click-by-click user experience, from the time they saw an advertisement on Facebook to the summary they would get after completing their class (manana); and directed a team of three coders to code the product in four weeks to get immediate user feedback (nididhyasana).

This framework works for every subject.

I continued using it for growing WhiteHat Jr, compressing my learning time for understanding new fields such as gamification and communities.

Founder's Growth = Company's Growth.

For the company to compress thirty years of growth into seven years, a founder has to compress their thirty years of learning into seven years.

The Vedantic learning framework will be your 30x7 learning guide.

Your 30x7 Execution—10x Thinking

Fifteen months into WhiteHat Jr in November 2019, we'd settled into a comfort zone. We'd raised Series A funding of Rs 70 crore ($10 million) in June 2019. We were improving the curriculum, building new technical features, and growing our marketing and sales teams. The company was growing at a predictable 20 per cent month-on-month when one day, while meditating on the commute to office, I had a sinking sensation in my gut. The vague feeling of unease I'd felt after our Series A funding got deposited in the company's bank account crystallized in my mind.

We were becoming a corporate entity.

The daily life-or-death fire to survive had been replaced by the warm glow of early success. Earlier, we had a 10x goal of creating a new category of live coding from scratch in the world, so we were working non-stop to understand how to make it more exciting for kids, how to explain the benefits to parents, and how to set up a large-scale live classroom operation. Now, with initial signs of the category being formed, we'd settled into a comfortable goal of growing at a normal pace and were making only incremental changes to the product daily.

We had to think 10x again. I called my leadership team of twenty members together.

We dug deep. Everyone shared the same 30x7 urgency to compress thirty years of learning and growth into seven years. We all believed in the mission of kids as builders and creators for life. No one wanted to settle into corporate complacency, even though we grudgingly admitted enjoying the brief reprieve from the 10x10x6 schedule.

We set a 10x goal again. We'd double each month and create the category all over the world. To do this, we had to execute three things immediately:

1. Launch in the US.
2. Set a stable systems and technology layer.
3. Create strong management structures.

Our US launch with higher margins would make us profitable, which would allow us to grow without slowing down for external funding. Our systems were set for stable, moderate expansion right then. In order to grow at the pace that we had envisioned, we'd have to make the technical architecture stronger so that we didn't have system crashes as more users came into the platform, and we could integrate new sales and customer support software easily with our database. Finally, growth meant more teachers and sales and operations employees, and since we wouldn't have new funding to make C-level hires, this meant that our current leaders would have to step up to lead larger teams.

We got to work. Within three months, we had launched in the US. The company turned profitable with the US customers reacting positively to the product. Our technology team took a decision to deprecate the old database, which was written with scrappy, early-stage code, and support the now-global operation with a new, elegant database. We migrated 100,000 customers to the new database over New Year's Eve in 2020 and slept at our office over the first week of the new year to manage the transition issues. With the new database in place, we quickly integrated support systems like Salesforce, Zendesk, Talkdesk and Exotel to improve our sales and customer services. Earlier, we'd be stuck in analyses-paralyses for days for decisions such as which software to install. Now, we made decisions within hours, understanding that executing a decision perfectly was more important than making the perfect decision. We were ready to scale.

We promoted strong middle managers to senior leadership within the company. From leading teams of twenty, they went on to lead teams of 150 people each. We coached them on leadership and training informally. Everyone did their best to step up to the challenge. For the next six months, WhiteHat Jr doubled each month. We didn't have new funding or management. Only a 10x goal.

I made several mistakes during this period, which I'd go back and correct. We set up strong technical systems to ensure that our customer experience remained excellent, but we should've done better with setting compliance processes for every small part of the company's operations. Our social media creatives went unregulated, published without review by a junior marketing team, which caused damage to the company's reputation. I should've hired a human resources head at 100 full-time employees and a dedicated head of culture at 300 employees. Instead, I hired them when we had more than 500 and 3,000 employees, respectively, which led to the weakening of the company's fabric.

I wouldn't attribute these mistakes to setting a 10x goal as much as to my own failure in not understanding how to run an organization of this scale. The largest team I'd run before was 250 members as head of Discovery India. Now, I was running a team of 5,000 employees and 12,000 teachers. If I were to do it again, I would set the same 10x goal but prepare myself better for the transition.

You can do your 10x planning better than me but always plan 10x for your ownership idea. You'll set up new systems to execute your goals and your time will expand to fill your goals. It works in business and in life.

10X

I didn't know this concept back in 2006, but I had an intuitive sense that my goals were too small. Like all my colleagues, I wanted to do well at Procter & Gamble, my first job, and be promoted faster than others. One day, I was at an office dinner in Cincinnati where everyone was talking about renovating their new houses, planning their next vacation, and their favourite television shows and restaurants. I felt an emptiness well up within me. There had to be more to life than comparing notes on television shows and restaurants. I just didn't know what. I'd been an avid reader all my life, so I thought I'd write a book to fill my growing vacuum. I set a goal of completing my first novel in six months.

My time expanded to fulfil my goal.

Before I started my novel, I had a restless, unfocused energy on weekends or after work, discussing office politics, watching Bollywood movies, playing a bit of tennis or cricket, none of it adding to mastery in any field. Now, I wrote my book for four hours each Saturday and Sunday and one hour daily after work. I wouldn't stop until I met my goal of 400 words per day on weekdays and 1,000 words each day on weekends. Within six months, I completed *Keep Off the Grass*.

For the first time, I experienced that your time, capability, or resources don't need to expand to succeed. Only your goals do.

30x7 in Your Day Job

Are you not yet ready to take the ownership plunge?

You can start following the 30x7 principle in your day job immediately. Corporate careers give a few 30x7 growth opportunities that your own venture can't:

A. New geographies
B. New industries
C. Turning your hobbies into mastery

I moved from India to the Philippines, Singapore and the US early in my career, working on local consumer brands in each market, solidifying my thesis that people around the world were more similar than different. Without this experience, I wouldn't have conceptualized WhiteHat Jr as a global company from the start. In moving industries from consumer goods to management consulting and then media, I learnt that the fundamental building block of success in every industry is the same. You just have to know your user well and create a product ten times superior to what they'd experienced before. Without this, you won't succeed in any industry. As a result, I micromanaged every detail in the first version of the WhiteHat Jr product. Every user touchpoint, from scheduling classes to their experience with the teachers, had to be ten times superior to classes in the physical world for the product to be accepted. The learning from shifting geographies and industries in my corporate career was useful daily in the start-up. But I was most transformed—and WhiteHat Jr was most impacted—by the pursuit of mastery in my hobbies.

Without the steady rhythm of a corporate job, I couldn't have gone deep into writing novels, hiking or yoga. As a result, I wouldn't have experienced the personal transformation that's inevitable in the pursuit of mastery in any field. As Eugen Herrigel says in *Zen in the Art of Archery* (1948):

> I must only warn you of one thing. You will become a different person in the course of these years. For that is what the art of archery means: a profound and far-reaching contest of the archer with himself. Perhaps you have hardly noticed it yet but you will feel it very strongly when you meet friends and acquaintances again in your own country; things will no longer harmonize as before. You will see with different eyes and measure with different measures. It has happened to me too, and it happens to all who are touched by the spirit of this art.

In the lonely early days of WhiteHat Jr when I'd often regret shifting from the head of Discovery where I called on CEOs and state officials to now having my phone call cut by customers sixty or seventy times a day, I'd take comfort from my writing days. You start with a blank page when you decide and sit to write. Only a dream that one day you'll turn it into a 300-page novel that people will actually read keeps you going for years. Rejections pile up. Friends, family, everyone loses confidence in you. Yet you keep writing, revising and rewriting for years because you believe. I'd experienced the same in tough hikes like to Kilimanjaro in Africa, where you feel you have nothing left to give yet you dig in deep to make an attempt at the peak. Or in the Sivananda Ashram, where I slept in a bare dormitory for months, took cold showers daily, and often fell on my head when I practised the asanas, in the hope that I'd master yoga one day.

I reminded myself I had to do the same at WhiteHat Jr. Just show up daily. The output was not in my control, but the input was. All I owed life was the gift of 100 per cent energy to my input daily. Once you pursue mastery in any field, you just learn to show up and give it all to your input, without letting your motivation flag.

Now, it's your turn.

Exercise Number 4: How to Start your 30x7 Journey.

1. Prepare for ownership in the next 120 days:

- Sravana: Read and/or listen to all the highly rated books, blogs and podcasts in your ownership field in the next ninety days.

- Manana: Formulate your plan for the first version of your ownership idea, such as an outline for your book or the wireframe for your product, in the next fourteen days.
- Nididhyasana: Dive into execution—write the first chapter of your book or start coding the first version of your product in the final fourteen-day sprint.

2. Set a 10x goal for your ownership idea:

- What would you do with your ownership idea if resources weren't a constraint?
- Now, what steps can you take to execute the above with the resources that you have?

3. If you're not ready to be an owner of your product yet, can you do any of these immediately:

- Shift to a new geography with your current job or change jobs to experience a new industry altogether?

And/Or

- Transform your hobby into mastery, such as turning your interest in reading into writing a book, music into composing an album, and hiking into scaling a difficult mountain?

'The Yogi is superior to the ascetics and even superior to the men of knowledge. The Yogi is also superior to those who perform action with interested motive. Therefore, O Arjuna, be thou a Yogi, yes Arjuna, be thou a Yogi.'

—Lord Krishna, the Bhagavadgita

5

Your Daily '1,1,1' Routine

START-UPS cross one valley of death after another in their path to success. Every time you cross a phase, a new dark storm threatens to destroy you because the people and processes you need for the next phase are different from what you had needed in the previous phase. The engineering head, who helped you succeed in the prototype phase with quick, scrappy code, for instance, becomes a liability for the next phase when hastily written code can cause debilitating customer experience issues. You need to hire a strong chief technology officer fast.

The same urgency repeats across functions. Since the phases are coming and going in such quick succession, your leaders and processes become antiquated almost as fast as you set them. As a result, so many things can go wrong for a start-up despite your best intentions, and hence only 17,000 companies out of 28 million survive to become full-fledged organizations that generate more than $50 million of revenue (see Figure 5.1).[1] Our darkest storm came when it seemed we'd crossed all the valleys of death successfully.

Figure 5.1: The start-up valley of death

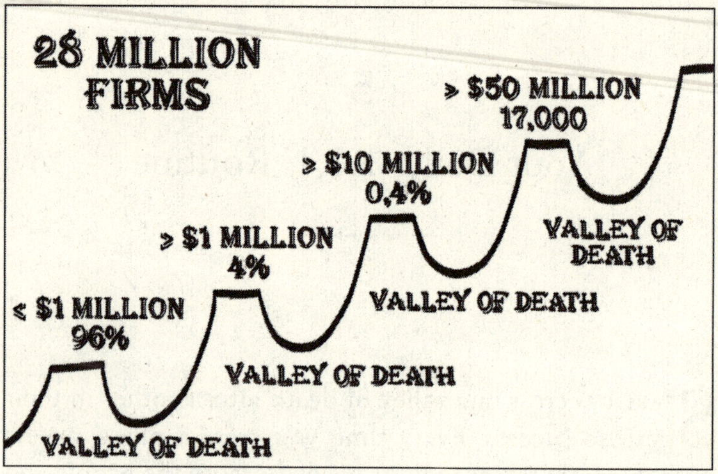

Source: Verne Harnish, *Scaling Up*

From a low-profile brand with a loyal following, WhiteHat Jr was suddenly thrust into the limelight with the acquisition by BYJU's, India's largest education technology company, in August 2020. The media wrote breathless articles about the $300 million, all-cash deal, a record of sorts in India for an eighteen-month-old company. Investors and entrepreneurs alike celebrated the glimmer of hope in the middle of the COVID-19 pandemic. Our team was excited. Beyond individual financial gains, everyone was excited that BYJU's education expertise would take the mission of kids as creators from coding to mathematics and from India to all over the world. Just a few days after the acquisition, however, everyone turned against us with the same frenzy.

Our marketing team had done a social-media campaign six months before the acquisition, which may've been considered funny for a young start-up but was in poor taste for the mature education company we were considered post-acquisition. We paid the price for our junior team and poor marketing compliance in our early phase. The creatives were plastered all over the Internet. We overreacted in the media, thinking that the backlash was a targeted act, since nine or ten creatives out of more than 1,000 that the company had done were being posted everywhere—and that too from six months ago.

People cast aspersions on the quality of our teachers. We'd been particularly respectful of our teachers since the start of the company. My mother was an army officer's wife, and despite being a Delhi University topper, she'd never been able to build her independent career because of my father's frequent transfers. Like her, hundreds of thousands of highly educated, qualified Indian women didn't participate in the workforce, whether from primary childcare responsibilities or their inability to commute at odd times to offices due to safety issues, or because of transferring with their husbands in military and government jobs. Women represented 21 per cent of India's workforce despite being half of college graduates in the country, placing India in the bottom ten countries in the world in terms of women workforce participation. In contrast, similar economies such as China and Brazil had 61 per cent and 48 per cent of women in the workforce, respectively. We envisioned empathetic, highly qualified women from India becoming teachers for the world through our live online model. The vision was coming to life with more than 12,000 teachers on the platform doing over 40,000 live classes daily, with the average class ratings being staggeringly high at 4.8/5 across India, the US, the UK and Australia. Students from all over the world loved their teachers in India. We reacted strongly to teachers being disrespected and battled every accusation, which did nothing but feed the media storm.

In hindsight, we should've just kept making our compliance and operational systems stronger instead of overreacting. It was a negative, distracting phase for the company.

Right in the middle, in November 2020, we had a family medical situation. My wife and I moved with our kids to Florida in the US to be with my wife's parents. For three months, I stayed up all night leading the business with our team in India, then handled media enquiries and accusations in the early morning hours, and later spent the afternoon teaching my kids, as they were in a different time zone from their online school in India.

At 5 p.m., I'd sleep for four hours until 9 p.m. when I would wake to complete my daily routine on time for our daily management meeting in India. I wouldn't recommend four hours of sleep for extended periods to anyone, nor was my decision-making quality at its best, as evidenced by my missteps in handling the negative press. But my energy never flagged during this period. I woke up daily at the start of the India workday, energized to give my all to creating new courses and launching in new markets, then vigorously defended the company in media interviews, and later, rarely felt rushed or short-tempered with my kids at the end of the US workday when I did their bath and meals.

The founder's energy drives the energy of the organization.

And we survived that Death Valley because our organization's energy remained high. We continued to be productive during this three-month phase. The organization rallied to launch a new brand for live coding and mathematics classes called BYJU's FutureSchool internationally, made our systems comply with the highest global standards, and launched our first live music offering where kids could learn piano and guitar in seven countries across the world simultaneously.

How do you always keep your energy high through the inevitable ups and downs of your 30x7 ownership phase?

My energy grew manifold after I incorporated the daily '1,1,1' routine in my life in 2013 when I first learned meditation. No matter how stretched I was, I committed daily to:

- Exercise: One hour
- Meditation: One hour (thirty minutes in the morning as soon as I got up; 30 thirty in the night just before sleeping)
- Reading/Reflection: One hour

I've rarely missed a day of following this '1,1,1' routine in the last decade. Even when we moved to the US in November 2020, I kept the routine going—exercising at 9 p.m. US time, keeping the same time as my 7.30 a.m. exercise schedule in India; meditating just before sleeping at night and after waking up in the morning as I did in India; and reading and reflecting on a new topic at the end of the workday. The energy from the routine preserved my sanity while I did a double shift daily for three months, working full hours on India time and spending full time with family on US time.

'1,1,1,' ROUTINE

Exercise: One Hour

Eighty per cent of people break their new year's exercise resolutions by February.[2] They can't keep themselves motivated mainly because they set vague goals—for example, 'I should exercise more'—or they can't find space for exercise in their daily routine.

Set a specific goal for your exercise—'I will exercise sixty minutes daily except Sunday.' Then, balance the opposing forces of routine and variation to create a daily exercise rhythm:

Routine

Exercise at the same time daily, ideally at home or a place close to home, so that your mind considers exercise as much of a habit as brushing your teeth or walking your dog. I've always exercised from 7.30 to 8.30 a.m., for instance, mostly at home with yoga and weights, or running close to home. Even on the US trip, I didn't break this pattern despite the time difference, so the mind never had to choose between doing exercise and not doing exercise on any given day.

Variation

Ensure enough variety within a week so that you don't get fatigued by repetition. For example, I alternate between running, weight training and yoga, each for two days a week.

Exercise is a remarkable gift. Your body will often feel tired in your hectic 30x7 ownership schedule, but exercising daily, even on days when every cell of your body is screaming against a workout, will immediately give you an energy lift. Balance routine and variation to never miss your daily one-hour exercise, taking just one break day per week to rest your body.

Meditation: One Hour

My favourite definition of meditation comes from Patanjali's Yoga Sutras.

Meditation is *chitta vritti nirodha*.

Meditation stills the restless thought waves of the mind.

I don't think I was capable of any great endeavour prior to starting meditation in 2013. Daily, I would lose tremendous energy from restless, uncontrollable waves of thoughts. I was hasty and impatient in meetings, cutting people off, looking to get to the next point faster. My sleep at night was often disturbed. I was rarely fulfilled in personal relationships as I was always looking to be more, do more, experience more.

Meditation was the greatest boon in my life, even though I didn't start meditation as a productivity tool. I wanted a transcendental insight into the nature of reality after my mother's death in August 2010 and widely read accounts of people having a direct experience with the universal consciousness without the intermediary of organized religion. From the Dhammapada in Buddhism to the Upanishads in Hinduism and the Kabbalah in Judaism, I read mystic accounts in books through all of 2011. Meditation was the underlying strand across all mystic texts. I started meditating in 2012 but developed a consistent practice only in 2013 when I did two ten-day silent Vipassana retreats one after the other during our sabbatical, starting with Dhamma Aṭala, a Vipassana meditation centre in Lutirano, a small village near Florence in Italy, where we stopped on our way from Scotland to Turkey by road. The centre was in the middle of a beautiful valley that was surrounded by lush mountains on all sides. But we had little time to appreciate the views as we were immediately put to work on the day we arrived. We would follow a rigorous schedule for the next ten days (see Table 5.1):

Table 5.1: Vipassana daily schedule

4.00 a.m.	Wake-up bell
4.30–6.30 a.m.	Morning meditation
6.30–8.00 a.m.	Breakfast break
8.00–11.00 a.m.	Meditation
11.00 a.m.–12.00 p.m.	Lunch break
12.00–1.00 p.m.	Rest
1.00–5.00 p.m.	Meditation

5.00–6.00 p.m.	Break
6.00–7.00 p.m.	Meditation
7.00–8.15 p.m.	Teacher discourse
8.15–9.00 p.m.	Meditation
9.00–9.30 p.m.	Question–answer session with teacher
9.30 p.m.	Lights out

Source: www.dhamma.org/code

Barring a few short breaks, we would meditate for the whole day. You had to maintain complete verbal and written silence during this period; you were allowed access neither to your phone nor to the Internet. Food was restricted to a light breakfast and lunch so that you didn't feel heavy while meditating. You couldn't exercise or read. For twelve hours a day, you focused only on meditation without distraction.

I wasn't intimidated by the schedule. I'd been looking forward to focusing single-mindedly on meditation and putting my theoretical knowledge gathered over reading tens of books into practice. However, from the first hour itself, I felt myself overcome by restless thoughts. My girlfriend and I had just got engaged. I rehearsed in my mind how I'd tell our families that we didn't want to have a conventional wedding because we didn't like the pomp and waste of it. My father had had one heart attack two decades ago, which never repeated, but I would constantly worry that he would have another one during this ten-day period when I was out of touch. I circulated through the plots and characters of my third novel in my mind. For the next ten days, I seemed to do everything except meditate. I was surprised by how restless and untrained my mind was, despite a year of reading books and trying to practise meditation.

I didn't get any glimpse of spiritual enlightenment during these ten days. Clearly, I wasn't ready. I had to double down on my practice. On the rest of our road trip, from Italy to Greece, then to Bulgaria and Turkey, I meditated in trains, buses and boats, for as many hours as I could without tiring. We did one more silent retreat immediately after arriving in India, in Kolhapur in Maharashtra, before our yoga teacher's training. I was calmer in this retreat but still no closer to any direct spiritual insight. However, I'd started to understand the theory of meditation viscerally from the back-to-back silent retreats and my own practice in between. This gave me the construct of the meditation practice I would continue for almost a decade after.

How to Meditate: Begin Your Concentration-Based Meditation Today

For beginners, I recommend a concentration-based meditation approach to make your mind one-pointed and prevent the familiar scattering of thoughts. Here's how to start:

Step 1: Select your object of concentration.
Step 2: Select your point of concentration.
Step 3: Start meditating.

How to Choose Your Object of Concentration

The three most common objects are:

- Your breath.
- An image—anything you feel some affinity for. For instance, I'm a big fan of the Buddha, so concentrating on his image worked for me in the beginning. My friend is a musician who concentrates on his guitar.
- A mantra: You don't need a guru to give you a magic collection of words. Repeating any word or set of words that evoke a positive emotion—Om, Buddha, Amen—anything works.

You can choose multiple other objects—chakras, deities, vision boards and fabric patterns, for example. Just understand the basic construct: You are using an object as an aid to shift focus *away* from your many distracted thoughts *towards* one, focused object. The nature of the object is immaterial; anything that can hold your attention for some length of time works.

How to Choose Your Point of Concentration

A point of concentration will help improve your focus by zoning it into a smaller area:

- If you choose your breath: The area between your upper lips and the tip of your nostrils. Or the contraction and extension of your chest during inhalation and exhalation.
- If you choose an image: Visualize the image in the third eye (your forehead between the two eyes) if you

consider yourself more analytical than emotional or in the centre of your heart if it is the other way round.

- If you choose a mantra: Focus on your lips if you're saying it aloud or focus on either your heart or the space between your eyes, as above, if you're repeating it mentally.

How to Meditate

- Posture: A good meditation pose has only two characteristics: sthira (a pose of attention) and sukha (a pose of comfort). If you're sitting cross-legged on the floor and your mind is screaming in agony, it's not a good pose for you because it's not sukha. On the other hand, if you're lying on the bed, attempting to meditate, that is not likely to work as well since it's not sthira. So, choose anything—sitting on a chair, sitting on the bed with your legs stretched, or sitting on a cushion on the floor—anything that allows you to be both comfortable and attentive. Just keep your spine erect for attentiveness and your hips at an elevation to your knees for comfort.
- Meditate: Close your eyes to avoid all distractions, straighten your spine and concentrate on your chosen object at the point of concentration. You're meditating.
- Time: Thirty minutes every morning, thirty minutes every night. Every day. You'll see noticeable changes in your life almost immediately.
- Obstacles: Too many to list. There'll be some external ones—your kids waking up early, a late night at work—but mostly your mind plays havoc. 'He said that', 'She

failed me', 'They don't understand me', 'I don't like her', many-branched and endless are the thoughts of the unsteady mind. Don't give up. You're going to get better as you go.

What Are the Benefits of Meditation?

Meditation stills the restless thought waves of the mind, and you'll start to see the benefits of the practice almost immediately.

IMMEDIATE BENEFITS:

Your concentration will improve. On my return from our sabbatical in 2014, I was surprised to see myself mathematically calculating things much faster at work, for instance, as I hadn't expected skills like these to improve at the age of thirty-five. One day, I was reviewing Kraft's gum and candy global volume shipment forecast for 2015 with my team and kept answering the category president's questions on what was shipping from which plant by calculating the sum for the region by just looking at the slide on the screen, even as people were entering numbers in Excel files and hand calculators. Everybody, including me, was surprised. My concentration improved significantly in every project I did after I started meditating, both in my work and in my writing.

SHORT-TERM BENEFITS:

You'll sleep better in three months. I'd been a restless, impatient sleeper all my life, and would often stay awake before examinations in school and college, and later when I was about to make important presentations at work. Once, during a particularly bad phase in 2009 when my mother was dying of cancer and I was feeling stuck and anchorless in my management consulting job, I even used sleeping pills every few days to sleep. After three months of meditation, I started sleeping through the night. Now, after almost a decade of meditation, I can barely recall a handful of nights in the last decade when I've been unable to sleep from mental stress. My sleep remains undisturbed, no matter the context.

Long-Term Benefits

You'll experience noticeable changes in every part of life, from your personal and professional relationships improving to your diet changing, in six to twelve months. You'll be less hasty and more silent as you experience just a slight pause between being triggered by something and reacting to it. I was more patient at work and listened more rather than being directive, as I was earlier, because I could see the other person's earnestness in the pause. My diet changed, whether it was quitting coffee or becoming a vegetarian, because I became more aware of how food affected my mind and how I felt restless after my morning coffee and sluggish after my chicken sandwich lunch.

Far more personally important than the productivity benefits, meditation added profundity to my life. I better understood the spiritual texts I'd been reading for years. The strange emptiness I always felt, as if something indefinable was missing from my grasp, even in moments of great achievement, had a name, a cause and a cure now. I still haven't experienced the moment of enlightenment that I hoped I would when I started meditation, but I have an unshakeable sense that I'm a traveller on the right path.

Reading/Reflection: One Hour

I was able to start-up only because of my reading.

With an MBA straight after engineering, I didn't know anything about building a tech company, not even the basics such as the difference between tech and product hires, what was a full-stack engineer as against a front-end or a back-end engineer, and how to create a structurally solid database architecture. I went to a tech outsourcing company to build the first version of the WhiteHat Jr product. They gave me a timeline of three months and an estimate of Rs 50 lakh. I wanted to sign off to get the company off the ground but felt a discomfort in my gut. I was making a decision out of fear. I'd dreamt of building a tech company. I couldn't outsource tech. I had to bite the bullet and get over my fear. Over the next month, I studied seventy books on building start-ups, hiring and inspiring the best tech talent and the fundamentals of product management. I became the first product leader of the company, so I understood each detail of the product myself, rather than hiring one, as the venture capitalists were guiding me to. Instead of outsourcing tech, I studied enough about coding to ask technical questions in interviews to select an engineering manager, a front-end and a back-end engineer myself. We built the first product in-house in four weeks at a fraction of the cost quoted by the outsourcing agency. Just through reading and reflecting on my reading, I understood the basic framework of building a tech company, which allowed us to scale rapidly later. We would have probably gone under if we had moved with the slow speed of an outsourced tech set-up.

Later in WhiteHat Jr, even during the busiest times, I kept up my daily routine of spending one hour on reading and reflection. I typically split my reading during a given week into two categories:

- Eighty per cent focused power reading: I chose a subject to master, as I did with technology, and read every well-rated book, blog or podcast about the subject. I'd done the same with passive income, yoga and writing when I was pursuing these obsessively.
- Twenty per cent perennial literature: For a smaller proportion of my reading time, I read and reread *Satipatthana: The Direct Path to Realization* by Bhikku Analayo, *Buddha* by Karen Armstrong, *The Yoga Sutras of Patanjali* by B.K.S. Iyengar, *Vivekacudamani of Sri Sankaracarya* by Swami Madhavananda, *The Complete Bhagavad Gita: A Commentary* by Swami Satchidananda, and other such perennial texts to always have a current of calm, positive thoughts running in my life.

Subject-specific power reading balanced with perennial, spiritual texts charges me with the energy of new ideas but also ensures that I'm calm enough to not go off the deep end with my usual obsessive personality and start directing my teams in new directions daily!

One Easy Routine for Busy People: How to Integrate the '1,1,1' Routine in Your Life

At first glance, three hours a day devoted to self-care appears daunting. I'd made the mistake of slipping from this '1,1,1' routine and skipping meditation and reading at one particularly busy time during my six-month notice period at Discovery, when I was running the company in the day and executing WhiteHat Jr at night. I quickly observed my energy levels dip. My usual optimism gave way to excessive rumination on how tough everything was and a growing self-doubt on my ability to pull off the start-up. One day in October 2018, three months after I'd started, I even spoke to my wife about giving up on WhiteHat Jr and withdrawing my resignation from Discovery. But better sense prevailed, and I restarted the '1,1,1' routine. Here is how I integrated the '1,1,1' routine into a typical '10x10x6' start-up day (see Table 5.2):

Table 5.2: Daily '1,1,1' routine during start-up days

7.30–8.30 a.m.	Wake up and exercise immediately
8.30–9.30 a.m.	Time with kids/family
9.30–10.00 a.m.	Meditate on way to the office in an Uber (I know meditating in transit is a peculiar choice, but busy times lead to creative measures!)

10.00 a.m. –10.00 p.m.	Start-up
10.00–10.30 p.m.	Commute back home (I tried using it for reading/reflection but gave up after a bit to just check email from the day.)
10.30–11.30 p.m.	Read/reflect
11.30–12.00 p.m.	Meditate before sleep

Source: Created by the author

I would caution that you need your family's support to make this schedule work during your temporary imbalance period of ownership. Both my children were born during my ownership period, my elder daughter in 2014 just as I was deciding to become a full-time writer and my younger daughter in 2016 when I'd become one. They grew up in New York and Mumbai in the seven-year period when I was a writer, a solo entrepreneur, Discovery head and finally, WhiteHat Jr founder. Kerry, my wife, was the primary caregiver for our kids during this period, and though we never lived close to family who could support us, we had a nanny in India.

My parenting role was limited to the hour I had each weekday before the kids left for school and four dedicated hours on Sunday morning after my work week. I made every moment of this time count. My kids and I connected over learning the Hindi alphabet and maths problems on weekdays. On Sundays, I'd take them to the neighbourhood park in Mumbai, attentive to their needs, learning about their unique identity as individuals, whether it was my elder daughter Leela's fearlessness in making friends with squirrels and street dogs or my younger daughter Rumi's love for numbers as she counted the number of cars of the same colour we passed when we went to the park in an autorickshaw.

Did I miss their childhood in these seven years of single-minded obsession?

I don't know. My kids still have memories of swinging in the Andheri West playground we would visit and the dosa lunch after from the start-up days. Now, after the WhiteHat Jr exit, I have more time with my kids, but they don't seem to know the difference. Perhaps the daily life-or-death urgency of a 10x goal makes you come alive in every part of your fibre, making all senses alert, every moment deep. Or perhaps I did miss out on their formative years. I'll never know. I wish there was a way to balance both work and life but given a choice I would still choose temporary work–life imbalance for a lifetime of balance later. And support it with the '1,1,1' routine to stay healthy during this period.

An Unconscious Benefit of the Routine: '+2,=2,-2' Diet Improvement

I had an unexpected side-benefit from introducing the '1,1,1' daily routine in my life a decade ago.

My diet transformed.

I was always reasonably fit with a daily workout routine, but I became truly conscious of food's effect on my emotions almost immediately after starting this routine.

As part of my daily perennial reading, I read the Bhagavadgita where I learnt that all of nature, from inanimate objects to human personality, is built on three gunas or properties:

- Sattva: Purity and stillness
- Rajas: Activity and restlessness
- Tamas: Inertia and dullness

A river, still and pure, has the property of sattva, for instance. Storms are rajasic, while a rock is characterized by tamas, or heaviness and inertia. You see the same variations in human personality. The sattva-dominant personalities are still and calm in every situation, rajasic personalities are full of passion and energy, and tamas is the opposite of rajas, manifesting in procrastination and lack of ambition. We're all combinations of these elements and you become what you consume. That's why living in pure, still nature calms us while living in cities, with its man-made energy of restlessness and movement, makes us rajasic. Similarly, the food you consume affects your personality.

From my daily meditation and biweekly yoga practice, I became increasingly aware of how my thoughts were shaping my diet. I made changes to increase the quantity of sattva or purity in my thoughts:

+2: Add Two Sattvic Foods—Green Vegetables and Green Juice

Sattva, the quality of purity and stillness, is best manifested in food in a fully vegetarian diet. On days I ate more salads and vegetables, I saw my yoga practice flow better, especially the backward bends, such as the bhujangasana or the cobra pose and dhanurasana or the bow pose. I'd always leaned towards vegetarianism but after starting the '1,1,1' routine, I turned 100 per cent vegetarian. I added four glasses of raw green juice with kale, broccoli, cucumber and celery daily, and ate salad and cooked vegetables in unlimited quantities for lunch and dinner. Immediately, I found myself lighter and more energetic through the day.

=2: Regulate Two Rajasic Foods—Coffee and Sugar

Any food that agitates you has rajas, the quality of passion and restless energy. During my thirty minutes of meditation each night, I observed how restless my thoughts were when I had coffee in the day or dessert in the evening. I switched from coffee to tea and turned processed sugar products into a weekend treat instead of a daily routine. Earlier, I would have a bar of chocolate or a carbonated soft drink once a day, and now I would have them a maximum of once a week as a treat. My sleep improved, my thoughts were steadier, and I no longer experienced the high sugar levels or caffeine-withdrawal crashes that I used to.

–2: Eliminate two Tamasic foods—Bread and Meat

I was most impacted when I had tamasic food, that is, food with the quality of inertia and dullness. Every time I had any meat for dinner, or even fish, I was hazy and dull during my nightly meditation. I couldn't do a headstand for longer than a minute or two if my lunch was heavy with roti or rice. First, I eliminated all meat from my diet, and then, I replaced toast with green juice at breakfast and roti with brown rice at dinner. Later, I kept following my body's guidance and just ate cooked vegetables and daal without accompanying rice for dinner. A fog seemed to lift from my mind. I felt lighter and more focused at thirty-five than I'd felt years ago when I'd just started my career as a twenty-three year old.

None of the above changes were a conscious attempt to improve my health or lose weight. I was just following what I was learning in reading and experiencing in my daily exercise and meditation. The +2,=2,–2, diet became a part of my life. Without trying, I lost 20 kilograms within a year. All the aches and pains I'd accepted as signs of ageing in my body, whether it was the crippling pain in my knee during running or my lower back pain after a long workday, disappeared. The steady stream of light, focused energy in my body and mind transformed both the clarity and quantity of my output.

Your '1,1,1' routine too will work in unexpected positive ways.

Now, it's your turn.

Exercise Number 5: Begin Your '1,1,1' Routine Today!

Create a daily one-hour exercise routine:

1. Block the same time to exercise daily (routine).

- Do at least two types of exercise over six days, for example, weights and running or running and yoga, while keeping the seventh day one of rest (variation).

2. Start your concentration-based meditation practice today:

- Step 1: Select an object of concentration you're pulled towards.
- Step 2: Select your point of concentration—third-eye region (forehead between the eyes) if you're analytical or the centre of your heart if you're emotional.
- Step 3: Meditate for thirty minutes in the morning as soon as you wake up and thirty minutes before you sleep at night.

3. Read/reflect daily starting today:

- Power reading: Read all highly reviewed books, blogs and podcasts for the ownership project you're working on. If you're looking for recommendations, Chapter 8 of this book has my selection of seven books that helped me in my ownership journey.
- Perennial literature: Select three to five spiritual classics and keep reading and rereading a few pages daily to always have a calm, positive energy in your life. My five most impactful reads in this genre are:
  1. *Sattipathana: The Direct Path to Realization* by Bhikku Analayo.
  2. *Buddha* by Karen Armstrong.
  3. *The Yoga Sutras of Patanjali* by B.K.S. Iyengar.
  4. *Vivekacudamani of Sri Sankaracarya* by Swami Madhavananda.
  5. *The Complete Bhagavad Gita: A Commentary* by Swami Satchidananda.

'Worst of all, continual fear, and danger of violent death: and the life of man, solitary, poor, nasty, brutish and short.'

—Thomas Hobbes, *Leviathan*

6

The '90 Per Cent Failing/100 Per Cent Learning' Rule

On the day in March 2018 when we received the first dismal television channel ratings of Discovery Jeet, the Discovery India general entertainment channel (GEC) I had conceptualized and led, I was forwarded a meme on WhatsApp. The image showed Baba Ramdev, a wellness guru whose biopic was the channel's launch show, in an inverted yoga position with a caption that read 'Discovery Jeet: First from the Last'. I felt like someone had stabbed me in the gut. The Discovery team had worked on the channel non-stop for two years with deep conviction in our hearts. We wanted mainstream Indian television viewers to have an uplifting Discovery-esque alternative to supernatural dramas and long-stretching fictional soaps which dominated the primetime. The team of ten content executives I'd handpicked had mounted stories of real-life people from small towns who'd made it big, such as Baba Ramdev, in the soap-operatic style loved by Indians. It was meant to be the birth of a new, inspiring fact-based fiction genre on Indian television. The audience rejected it. Noble intentions didn't matter on television. The shows were just not engaging enough.

I'd failed before with my novels, but this was my first public failure. A veteran Discovery India executive wrote a scathing article about me in a news column. When I dropped my children to school, strangers came up to me and told me that they always knew the channel would fail, and the parents who knew me at school averted their eyes, probably embarrassed to express their condolences. Competitors leaked stories to the press of how Discovery India was in turmoil since their first major bet in India in twenty years had failed. I slowly accustomed myself to the new world of social trolling and personal attacks. Failure is tough enough; the public condemnation that follows a notable failure makes the blow doubly hard.

And yet, no one can truly predict which way the coin will turn when you create. But the odds are that it'll flip to failure more often than to success. In observing three creation industries up close and personal—writing, media and start-ups—I saw similar statistics. Ninety per cent of books fail, 90 per cent of new television channels lose money[1] and 90 per cent of start-ups shut down within five years.[2] The probability of success in all creation industries is less than 10 per cent.

Creation lies at the edges of the system, never at the centre of it. You're solving a problem that hasn't been articulated. No one is asking for your solution yet. Can any expert or commentator foresee whether your idea will make it to the centre? I don't think so. Why else would the top twelve children's publishers reject Harry Potter[3] and seven prominent investors of Silicon Valley pass on AirBnB?[4]

Even the cliches of hard work and success don't always hold true. *Keep Off the Grass*, which I wrote part-time for an hour daily after work over six months as a debutant, without reading any books on writing or taking any writing classes, struck a chord with the audience. HarperCollins India published only 5,000 copies of the book in the first print run in June 2008, a nominal figure for a new author in India. It sold out within a month. Then, they published another 5,000 copies. It sold out within two weeks. The buzz on college campuses across India was so high that the book kept going out of stock almost as soon as new copies were published. Within the next few years, the book would go on to sell 60,000 copies, exceeding all projections of HarperCollins India. In contrast, I wrote *The Seeker* over three years of full-time writing, having read hundreds of books to improve my craft and after doing extensive research to make every detail accurate in the novel. The novel received rave reviews from experts. Yet, Penguin Random House struggled to sell even their first print run of 25,000 copies in India.

Can you articulate the inarticulable?

There's a 90 per cent chance you won't.

Why risk it all at such low odds of success then?

Because your success probability is 10 per cent but your learning probability is 100 per cent. Failure is discrete but learning from each failure compounds until one day, one idea will work.

The '90 Per Cent Failure, 100 Per Cent Learning' Rule

Here's a chart of my ownership endeavours in the last decade (see Table 6.1):

Table 6.1: Personal creative success rate

Year	Project	Results	Full-time/ Part-time
2008	Book: *Keep Off the Grass*	Major bestseller	Part-time
2010	Book: *Johnny Gone Down*	Above average bestseller	Part-time
2015	Book: *The Seeker*	Failed	Full-time
2018	TV: New channel launch—Discovery Jeet	Failed	Full-time
2018	TV: New Discovery Kids channel launch—Little Singham	Major success (but 'kids' is a small category overall)	Full-time
2020	Start-up: New company launch (WhiteHat Jr)	Successful exit	Full-time

Source: Created by the author

My overall success rate is 33 per cent. The success rate falls to 25 per cent among four full-time ownership projects. And my success rate was zero for the first two full-time projects.

90% FAILURE/100% LEARNING

The more chances you take, the luckier you get. Your learning from each experience compounds. Your success probability for your first creative project may be 10 per cent but your growth and self-transformation probability is 100 per cent. As a result, the person attempting the next project is a fundamentally different, improved person who has a higher success probability the next time over.

On the surface, I had nothing to show, for example, from two back-to-back failures with *The Seeker* and Discovery Jeet. I was devastated both times, and my first reaction was to blame it on hard luck. After a week of grieving, however, I was ruthless about analysing why I failed. Discovery Jeet failed because our content wasn't ten times better than the established general entertainment channels' competition content, even though our shows had excellent user feedback in concept research. Out of the 197 million Indian households owning television sets, close to 98 per cent had just one television set,[5] so television viewing was a family activity in India. In concept testing, viewers were excited to see cinematic biopics on television during 8 p.m. to 9 p.m. in prime time so that their children could be inspired while their elderly parents were pulled into the dramatic human conflicts that the heroes and heroines of the biopics overcame to reach their goal. However, concept research didn't test for execution. Daily television covers its costs by amortizing one-time sets and production costs over a large number of episodes. To make our economics work, we stretched the fact-based stories that should've been told in four tight one-hour episodes into sixty watered-down thirty-minute episodes. Our competitive television channels also stretched their stories, but fictional narratives allowed them to introduce as bizarre a plot twist as it took to keep users hooked to the shows. One popular show, for example, had a woman turn into a snake in the middle of the show to liven things up. They made interesting television. Our stories were good but not ten times more engaging. Your product has to be ten times better as a new entrant to break user habit. We failed as a result, and the buck stopped squarely at me.

I'd set a compelling fact-based fiction vision, but I'd never done television content before, so I let our content team make all decisions about the pacing of shows, the number of episodes, and the key dramatic points in each episode. They, in turn, had been sincere about delivering the vision, but handicapped by the pressure to stretch the stories. Content was core in a television channel, and I should've read scripts of the key shows before green-lighting them. My lack of experience in television script evaluation was not an excuse. A leader has to become an expert in everything that matters in their company. I'd been focused on the wrong things—marketing, strategy, finance, advertising sales, channel distribution—which merely supported the content creation.

At WhiteHat Jr, therefore, I was deeply involved with the product right from the first day. In the early days, I reviewed every curriculum lesson twice across all grades with the curriculum creators, sat for hours with kids who came to our office every weekend to give product UX feedback and set up rigorous user experience tracking after every class. Despite knowing nothing about technology, I read so many books and blogs that I was able to weigh in on database architecture and syntax choices with the coders in our team. No one in my core team minded my meddling. The best people feel a heightened sense of pride in their work when a leader is involved in the deepest details to delight a user. Only insecure folks consider it to be micromanagement. Kids loved the WhiteHat Jr product from the start, as a result, and that allowed us to create the category fast.

Without Discovery Jeet's failure, I would've continued my hands-off corporate management style, which works in big brands where you're pushing a wheel that's already turning, but not when you're creating a new wheel from scratch.

Neither were my three years spent writing *The Seeker* a write-off. I'd failed because the book's main theme of spiritual enlightenment was too intangible. This time, I ensured that our lofty vision—that kids would be lifelong builders and creators with WhiteHat Jr—was backed with tangible execution. Every child developed something real in each WhiteHat Jr course—prototype apps in coding, real-world project solutions in maths and their own compositions in music. Parents were eventually convinced to embrace the category both because their kids loved the classes and because kids were creating tangible markers of their learning in each class.

Your personal growth from a failed project *simply shows* in your next project. Learning compounds.

And your life will eventually be measured in 'decades not in days'.[6] The creator's life will be tough in the days. Your failures are celebrated after you become successful, but in the moment, they rip your life apart. You doubt yourself, everyone doubts you, your world is shattered. Following the Discovery Jeet failure, seven key Discovery India employees out of a total of 200 resigned to join other media companies because they thought the company was unstable. Competitors fed on the uncertainty and tried to poach more employees. I doubted my own abilities daily but I was fortunate to have the trust of both Discovery's international head and global CEO. They knew that India was a sub-scale business for Discovery with less than 1 per cent contribution to the company's global revenue, despite having more than 15 per cent of the world's population. Big swings had to be taken, and big swings in a creative business are accompanied by big failures. They'd respected my zeal in pitching ideas to grow in a crowded media space one after the other and not relenting until I took them to execution. I was already beating myself up daily for the Discovery Jeet failure, unforgiving with myself in analysing and presenting to them what I'd done wrong and how I would do things differently, so they didn't seem to see any point in beating me up more for it.

I took confidence from them and rallied the embattled organization by meeting most of the 200 employees in the company personally, listening to their fears and communicating my pride at us having the courage to take the risk to go from a niche network to mainstream. The organization's mood remained sombre. No one fully trusted me. We had to create things in the world again to get the momentum back. I gathered my courage and took another risk.

We had created a new kids' television show called *Little Singham*, based on the popular Bollywood cop character from the movie *Singham*. Once again, it was an inspiring, uplifting story, enveloped in a larger-than-life dramatic narrative, and I had tremendous conviction in it. I'd reviewed some surprising television ratings data on how children, unlike adults, loved repetition more than novelty. If they liked a character, they'd keep watching repeats of a show again and again instead of switching to a new show about a new character. However, Discovery had programmed the kids' channel like an adult channel for decades and rotated multiple shows around the clock to keep the channel fresh. I wanted to break this paradigm but second-guessed myself daily. I would lose complete credibility if another big move failed. And yet, I couldn't pay lip service to the organization that had the courage to take big risks when I was operating in selfish fear of my own reputation as a country head. I trusted my data-based instinct and stopped production on all our kids' shows to green-light 360 episodes of just *Little Singham*, a huge risk for a show that hadn't even aired once. Typically, a new kids' show on the channel would have a first production run of twenty-five episodes. Then, I made *Little Singham* 50 per cent of the Discovery Kids channel, with new shows for two hours in the afternoon and repeats running for the rest of the day. The remaining 50 per cent was run from new episodes and repeats of only one other show. Children only saw *Little Singham* and one other show on the whole channel. This unorthodox move catapulted the channel from the bottom of kids' television to the top three overnight. *Little Singham* became a cult hit among kids all over India. The organization's momentum improved.

A month later, we got confirmation from Prime Minister Narendra Modi that he would join *Man vs Wild*, a historic development in Discovery India's history since no sitting prime minister had featured in a Discovery television show before. Then, the Discovery global team green-lit a digital app which I'd been pitching for a year. I had reassured the organization—and myself—that we could rise again.

Life is hard in the days, but in the decades, the creator surges ahead from connecting the dots. Three decades of research by Korn Ferry[7] shows that learning agility is the single-best predictor of career success, not grades or college pedigrees. Learning-agile employees constantly seek new challenges at work, take risks and self-reflect from mistakes. They're obsessed with learning and growth rather than titles and promotions. As a result, they adapt quickly to unfamiliar situations and thrive among chaos and uncertainty, the number one most critical skill in a world changing dramatically from technology. The higher you go in an organization, the more you'll lead and make decisions in uncertainty. While ordinary careers stutter and plateau in this uncertainty, the learner's career accelerates.

Figure 6.1: The learner's career path

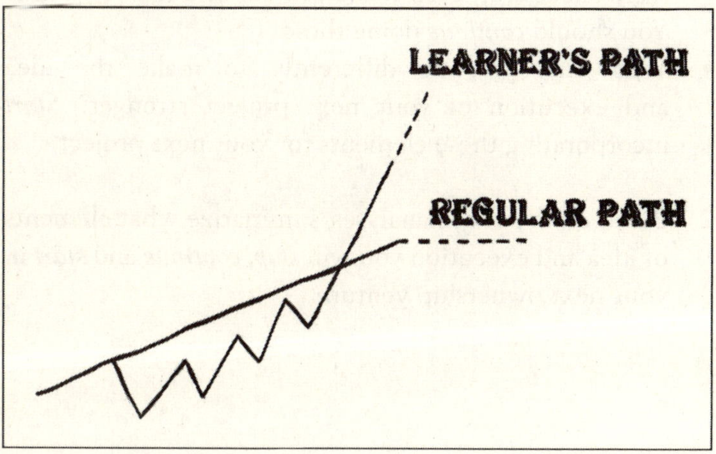

Source: Created by the author

Create. Learn. Create again. And one day, your probability of success will match your probability of learning at 100 per cent.

Now, it's your turn.

Exercise Number 6: Compound Your Learning from Your Failures Today

1. Make a list of your past failures. For each item on the list, write down:

- What elements of the project's idea and execution were unsuccessful? These are mistakes you should *stop* making.

- What elements of the project's idea and execution were successful, even if the project as a whole wasn't? You should *continue* doing these.
- What can you do differently to make the idea and execution of your next project stronger? *Start* incorporating these elements for your next project.

2. Based on the above analyses, summarize what elements of idea and execution you will *stop*, *continue* and *start* in your next ownership venture.

'The things you own end up owning you.'

—Chuck Palahniuk, *Fight Club*

7

'50/30/20' Investing Rule

My girlfriend and I stopped at one of my closest friends' place in London on our way from Scotland to Turkey by road during our 2013 sabbatical. He had just bought a new well-lit waterfront apartment with three rooms and large floor-to-ceiling windows in Canary Wharf, one of London's prime business districts. His wife was pregnant with their second child while their first kid was entering a prestigious private school. With a growing family, they wanted more space than they had had in their first apartment. They planned to put their old apartment on rent rather than sell it since London property values were expected to keep rising. He'd grown up in a small village near Bhopal in India and his family was proud of him, a homeowner settled in London.

I felt a pang of regret.

In college, my friend and I had a similar adventurous spirit, taking last-minute trips from Ranchi to Kathmandu via Raxaul by bus on a dime, and going by Royal Enfield motorcycles from Ladakh to Kanyakumari over an eight-week trip between engineering college and business school. Yet, here he was, working in a lucrative job, well established in family life, and owning not one but two houses in a prime real-estate market like London.

I, on the other hand, was unemployed, had never owned a house and was now about to sleep for a year in hostels, train stations and on the hard beds of an ashram dormitory.

Why wasn't I able to stop drifting aimlessly?

I would feel confused many times that year when I received pictures of my friends and cousins celebrating their kids' first day at school or buying a new house. Likewise, my sister and my then girlfriend Kerry's siblings had respectable corporate careers, lived comfortably in their homes in the US suburbs and had invested in second homes, which they had put on rent. Kerry and I were the black sheep in our families. I invested some of what I earned in equity markets, but the rest I spent on wandering. When would I 'grow up' and invest in houses and cars and build roots in one place?

Maybe never!

Back then, I didn't know these seven mental models for freedom. But subconsciously, I knew that my biggest investment early on in my career had to be in my own growth. Real estate would give nominal, predictable returns over the long term. Growing as an individual, however, could give outsized returns because it would completely change how I thought, worked and lived. Just like my growth during the first sabbatical had led to a bestselling novel, *Johnny Gone Down*, with a major movie deal and a significant acceleration in my corporate career.

I surrendered to the road for more growth.

How do you invest in your growth with your earnings?

I used the 50/30/20 allocation rule for my monthly salary.

50/30/20 Investing Rule

Invest your net take-home salary each month as follows:

- 50 per cent: Needs
- 30 per cent: Wants
- 20 per cent: Savings

50/30/20 RULE

The 50/30/20 rule originates from the 2005 book, *All Your Worth: The Ultimate Lifetime Money Plan*, written by US Senator Elizabeth Warren and her daughter, Amelia Warren Tyagi, and is applicable across cultures and contexts.[1]

Fifty Per Cent 'Needs': Make Growth a Need

Fifty per cent of your salary each month should be allocated to your essential needs, such as housing, transportation, food, utilities, school fees, insurance, healthcare and elderly parent support.

If you're among the fortunate few in the world who earn enough to spend less than 50 per cent of your earnings on your needs, don't save the remaining.

Spend it on personal growth in avenues such as paying a higher rent to live in the centre of the city, buying an online course to further your education and investing in creating your own YouTube channel or blog.

Your growth today will lead to a life of ownership tomorrow.

In 2002, I was transferred to Procter & Gamble's Asian headquarters in Singapore after completing my internship in India. Our office was near the centre of the city in Novena Square, but most of the Indians in Procter & Gamble, Singapore, lived in Yio Chu Kang, a suburb one hour away from office, to save money. We spent the weekdays after work commuting, first a walk from the office to the Singapore metro, then a thrity-minute train ride and finally, twenty minutes waiting for and riding a public bus. The weekends were consumed by watching Bollywood movies, cooking Indian food and playing cricket with other Procter & Gamble colleagues from India.

I grew very little during the year despite living in a new country.

One night, I was at the usual drunken party at a friend's place on a weekend when I caught myself discussing real-estate prices in Yio Chu Kang. I felt an emptiness well up within me. In the comfortable routine of life, I was taking on the goals and aspirations of people around me. I didn't want to buy houses or settle down. There had to be more to life. The next month, I moved alone to the centre of the city near Orchard Road, paying double the rent I was paying in the suburbs. My savings were lower, but my growth accelerated. My commute time after work was reduced to a few minutes against more than an hour as earlier, so I spent more time walking alone in Singapore's diverse neighbourhoods from Chinatown to Little Korea and Little India. As a result, I became more interested in Singapore's history and read about the country's remarkable transformation from being an island with no natural resources, which was banished from the Malaysian federation in 1965, to becoming the gleaming jewel of the East in the span of just one generation. One man, Lee Kuan Yew, Singapore's first prime minister, had shaped the destiny of an entire nation.

I too wanted my life to count more than just having a job and paying taxes. Now that I was at walking distance from Singapore's public library, I read more biographies and books in diverse fields such as politics, philosophy and history. I had a growing sense that I was living a small life, and jumped at any opportunity I got within Procter & Gamble to relocate to a new country. As a result, I moved with Procter & Gamble from Singapore to the Philippines for a few months in 2003, then back to Singapore, later to Cincinnati in the US in 2006 and Minneapolis in 2007, until one day I wanted to be even more unrestrained to travel. That's when I left to backpack full-time in 2008.

That one decision to break out of the pack and live in the centre of the city in Singapore led to my first sabbatical, which started my journey of ownership. I'd have saved more in the short term by living in the far suburbs, but I would not have grown enough to eventually write novels and do a start-up.

After Singapore, I always spent right up to the 50 per cent needs limit to live in the centre of every new place I moved to—Manila, Cincinnati, Minneapolis, Washington, DC, New York, back to Mumbai—and be at the centre of culture. I grew rapidly from that choice. In New York, for example, I could walk to museums like the Museum of Modern Art (MoMA) and the Frick Collection from my apartment. I'd never been a very visual person before, preferring to process information by words; now, for the first time, I found beauty and meaning in design. I trusted my instincts on visual art more. Later, this helped me create functional user experience (UX) and user interface (UI) quickly in WhiteHat Jr when we were a bootstrapped start-up with no designer.

Over the years, I also invested at various times in starting a blog, creating a YouTube channel, buying and reading hundreds of books, taking a Six Sigma Black Belt certification to sharpen my operational skills at work, and improving my writing with multiple writing courses. Growth was a need, and I became more and more comfortable investing the full 50 per cent limit in it.

Thirty Per Cent 'Wants': Choose Experiences over Possessions

In 2004, after I'd moved to my own apartment near Orchard Road, New Year's Eve was approaching fast and my heart sank at the thought of spending yet another new year drinking with friends in Sentosa Island. I'd spent three formative childhood years at a boarding school, Army Public School in Dagshai near Shimla, where we'd hiked extensively across the Himalayas. And lately, as part of my widening reading, I'd read non-fiction wilderness accounts such as Jon Krakauer's *Into the Wild* (1996) and *Into Thin Air: A Personal Account of the Mt. Everest Disaster* (1997), and Maurice Herzog's *Annapurna: The First Conquest of an 8000-Meter Peak* (1951). I was being pulled to the mountains again, so I decided at the last minute to go for a hike on New Year's Eve. I found a Chinese adventure group online who had an extra pass for hiking a mountain in Malaysia on New Year's Day. This must be a minor mountain since I can't even locate its name on an Internet search now. I bought the pass and went by bus from Singapore to Kuala Lumpur, and then to the base camp of the mountain to join them.

We started the twenty-four-hour non-stop hike at midnight on New Year's Eve, using headlamps to find our way through the thick foliage on the steep mountain. I hadn't hiked in more than a decade and struggled to keep pace with the avid Chinese hikers. I'd also not prepared well, thinking I would manage hiking easily since I was in good shape from my regular running. My drinking water ran out in the middle of the climb. People were loath to share their limited supplies of drinking water with me and I inched up like the walking dead, with my throat dry and my lungs exploding. I'd probably have got severely dehydrated but for running into a small stream halfway to the peak that I drank directly from, despite the Chinese guide advising me not to do so vigorously in sign language. I didn't have a choice.

We reached the peak without incident, even though my body shook like a leaf from fatigue while rappelling up and down the vertical rocks at the end. On the way down, I slipped and fell often but made it back to our bus parked at the park entrance, exactly twenty-four hours later at midnight on 2 January 2005.

It was a modest mountain, much smaller than the mountains which I would go on to climb later, like Kilimanjaro or multiple ranges in the Andes and the

Himalayas, but it had taken everything from me. I vowed to get back into hiking shape. On my bus trip back to Singapore, I felt a deep sense of contentment. This was life. Being in nature, pushing yourself to the brink and finding deep reserves within you to continue. I'd lost all sense of ego and self in the twenty-four hours of tough hiking. My petty, distracted thoughts about whether I'd get promoted fast from assistant brand manager to brand manager at work or whether my relationship at that time would work out had disappeared during the hike. I'd felt something spiritual in that silence and I wanted to experience it again.

From 2005, I turned into an avid hiker and used my savings to travel and climb tough mountains like Kilimanjaro in Africa, Volcán Tajumulco in Guatemala, Machu Picchu in Peru, Markha Valley in Ladakh and peaks all over the Himalayas and the Andes, often in sub-zero temperatures without guides.

It would be too pat to draw corporate or entrepreneurship lessons from a personal passion, but I do believe that I would have a fraction of the self-discipline and resilience I had during WhiteHat Jr's ups and downs or during *The Seeker*'s sixty rejections had it not been for hiking. I always knew you just had to show up every day, put one step in front of the other, and keep climbing. One day, you'll reach the peak.

Experiences trump possessions.

Years ago in 2006, I bought my first and only television set when I moved to the US. I had to pay for storing it when I went on my six-month international backpacking trip from the US, while the rest of my stuff just fit into two suitcases that I kept in my sister's basement in Maryland. Then, I paid to move it from Washington, DC, to New York. In my small New York apartment, it took up more than half of the space in the living room. And I found myself no richer for the thirty minutes I spent watching *Law & Order: Special Victims Unit* or the news on television daily. The deeper I was going into my reading and hiking, the more I was pulled towards content that inspired me to think and create against content that I consumed passively. I preferred to watch DVDs of classics like *Cinema Paradiso* (1988), *Apocalypse Now* (1979) and *Malcolm X* (1992), which I knew I could see equally well on my laptop because I cared very little about sound systems and image quality. Within a month of moving to New York, I sold my television. It was unnecessary baggage.

Experiences breathe and grow, while possessions deprecate and die.

Thirty per cent of your salary each month should be invested in your wants. Here are my top recommendations on 'want' investment experiences that are not only enjoyable but also will transform your self-discipline and creativity:

One week

Tough multi-day hikes. My top three picks: Kilimanjaro Machame Route, Machu Picchu Jungle Inca Trail and Markha Valley in Ladakh.

Two weeks

Ten-day silent Vipassana meditation retreat. You can visit the website www.dhamma.org to book your free retreat.

ONE MONTH

Residential thirty-day yoga teacher's training. Recommendation: Sivananda Yoga Teacher's Training held in multiple centres around the world.

Eight-hundred-kilometre Camino De Santiago hike from the Pyrenees in France to Santiago De Compostela in Spain.

THREE MONTHS OR MORE

Solo budget backpacking for three to twelve months, staying in hostels and cheap accommodations while crossing countries on buses, trains and boats. Recommended places: South America, Central Asia and East Europe, where the language and customs push you out of your comfort zone.

Twenty Per Cent Savings: Equity Investing 'Rule of Three'

In 2020, when WhiteHat Jr was growing fast, I asked my closest friend from London, whose place in Canary Wharf I'd stopped at during our sabbatical, to join me in the finance function. His banking career had plateaued in the uncertainty of Brexit and COVID-19. With the added threat of technology causing sweeping changes in traditional finance, he was increasingly fearful of becoming redundant in his investment banking job. He was tempted to join me, but with two houses in London and an additional investment property in Gurgaon, he was worried about the uncertainty of the start-up not working out. His savings were just not liquid enough to take the risk.

How do you use your savings to risk and grow?

First, invest in equity rather than real estate. From 2010 to 2020, US equity markets (Standard & Poor's [S&P]) generated about 13 per cent return[2] against real estate at 5 per cent.[3] Over even longer cycles, equity has always outperformed real estate in the US. Similarly, Indian equity markets over the long term generated an average of 14–16 per cent returns against real estate at 11 per cent.[4] More than returns, however, I've appreciated and preferred the one-click nature of entering and exiting equity investments to the complex paperwork, including mortgage pre-approvals, home inspections and appraisals, homeowner's insurance and closing, involved in buying and selling real estate. Why weigh yourself down with paperwork and transactions in a world of AirBnB and Housing.com? In my early forties now, I've never bought a house, which in a small way has liberated me to move geographies, industries and vocations at short notice, whenever I was inspired by an opportunity to grow.

Next, I've found the rule of three (discussed below) for equity investments helpful to keep my investments on autopilot, so I get returns equivalent to or better than the market, yet spend very little time on them. The time I save I invest in my own growth, whether in reading, deep-learning new things, or taking ownership plunges.

1. 100–Age Rule: Equity as Percentage of Your Total Portfolio = (100–Your Age)

I took a 90 per cent salary cut from Discovery to start WhiteHat Jr. Our household expenses exceeded my start-up salary. I covered the gap each month by selling the equities I held. During COVID-19, the markets crashed, and I couldn't sell stocks without wiping off my savings. So, I used the bonds and liquid cash reserves I kept at hand to meet our expenses and weather the storm.

Investing (100–your age) per cent of your total net worth in equity is a conservative guide to help you live through inevitable market cycles.[5]

For more aggressive risk takers like me, (120–your age) per cent is a good benchmark.[6]

At forty, when I started WhiteHat Jr, for instance, I had 80 per cent of my savings in equity. During COVID, I used the 20 per cent I held in cash and bonds to support our family's expenses. If I were twenty-five and without kids, I would perhaps have been able to survive mostly on my start-up salary and used 5 per cent cash and bonds to tide through the COVID crisis, keeping (120–25), that is, 95 per cent in equity investments untouched.

Your risk appetite should match your life stage and (100/120–your age) is a good benchmark for the equity percentage of your total portfolio.

Hands-On Domain Expertise Rule: Invest in Individual Stocks Only if You Have a Domain Advantage, Else Choose Index Funds

Eighty per cent of active fund managers who invest in individual stocks are unable to beat average stock index returns over a decade.[7] Warren Buffet famously advised that low-cost index funds, such as the S&P 500 Index Fund, with a representative basket of stocks from the whole economy, are your single best investing tool.[8]

Why invest one's time and energy in picking individual stocks when the best fund managers from the top schools in the world, who're working full-time on stock selection, are unable to beat the market?

Over the last fifteen years of equity investing, I invested only in index funds with just one exception—investing in companies and industries where I had hands-on domain expertise that I felt a fund manager couldn't replicate with theoretical analyses.

In 2006, for instance, I was working in brand marketing at Procter & Gamble in the US, when the company started experimenting with digital media for the first time. Initial results from Google's search advertising and YouTube's advertising platform were excellent, and I sensed that spend shifts from television to digital would become a widespread phenomenon for businesses all over the world. Hence, I invested in Google's stock in 2006 and Facebook's initial public offering (IPO) in 2012.

Similarly, I was living in New York in 2008 just as Amazon was expanding Amazon Prime. My retail store visits went down to zero with Prime's low prices and fast delivery. I figured this would become a trend outside the metros in the US and then, around the world, and invested in Amazon in its rapid expansion phase.

Google, Facebook, Amazon, which are 30 per cent of my portfolio, gave me outsized returns over the decade. The rest I invested in S&P 500 and NASDAQ (National Association of Securities Dealers Automated Quotations) index funds.

Are you seeing a company or industry emerge because of your unique front-row, hands-on vantage point?

Invest unhesitatingly in it, while putting the rest in index funds. Index funds will typically grow in the long term, and the passive nature of these investments allow you to put your active time in personal growth projects.

Ten Per Cent Allocation Rule: Don't Make Any Single Stock Greater than 10 Per Cent of Your Portfolio

I was so bullish on Facebook stock at one point, given how much advertising dollars were moving to digital, that I wanted to invest 25 per cent of my equity portfolio in Facebook alone.

Fortunately, I didn't.

Financial service companies[9] suggest a cap of 5 per cent on any investment to hedge your risks. For more aggressive risk takers, use a 10 per cent cap if you've found 'the one'.

The history of the world is replete with sure things collapsing, as I experienced personally when the Lehman Brothers collapsed in September 2008, triggering the US financial crisis which left me unemployed and broke on return from my sabbatical. The US economy had been considered a safe bet when I'd left for my sabbatical confidently in March 2008.

Facebook too has gone through tremendous ups and downs since its IPO, starting with its immediate crash after its debut in 2012 to the meteoric rise for years after, followed by the recent crash after the Meta rebranding. With the 10 per cent cap, I was never heavily leveraged in one stock and didn't waste time or energy tracking its daily movements.

With these three rules above, my investing returns in the last fifteen years of investing are 26 per cent on an annual basis against NASDAQ at 20 per cent in the same period.

I was never trying to beat the market, though. My goal was to have enough cushion to take six months off to backpack in 2008, then to learn yoga and meditation for a year in 2013, be a full-time writer for eighteen months in 2015 and finally, establish a start-up in 2018. I oriented my needs, wants and savings around this single thrust for growth.

Now, it's your turn.

Exercise Number 7: How will You Use Your Salary from Next Month?

Review your expenses over the last six months. What is your current break of needs/wants/savings?

1. **Needs**: Are you investing less than 50 per cent of your salary in your needs? Brainstorm three ideas on how you can increase your investment in growth. Examples include:

- Paying a higher rent to live in the centre of the city.
- Buying new books daily or taking online or physical courses in your interest areas.
- Starting your own blog or YouTube channel.

2. **Wants:** Are you investing 30 per cent of your salary each month in experiences over possessions? Brainstorm

three ideas on investing in experiences you've been dreaming of doing but putting off. Examples include:

- A week-long tough hiking trip.
- A ten-day Vipassana retreat or a thirty-day yoga teacher's training.
- Learning a musical instrument or joining a painting class.

3. **Savings:** Review your investment portfolio and identify areas where you can reallocate your investments step by step to enjoy the best returns and freedom in the long term using the following rules:

- Equity vs Real Estate Rule
- (100/120–Your Age) Rule
- Hands-on Domain Expertise Rule
- Ten Per Cent Single Stock Allocation Rule

PART II

A Step-by-Step Ownership Kit

Introduction: Let's Get Started

ONLY 2 per cent of Americans create art,[1] 98 per cent people consume art. Five per cent Indians are entrepreneurs,[2] 95 per cent work in organizations created by them. Only 20 per cent people in an organization are engaged enough in work to take ownership,[3] and on the other hand, 80 per cent people work enough to get by. Your choice to break out of the pack and be in the top 2 per cent, 5 per cent or 20 per cent, respectively, will be the most difficult choice in your life, and ultimately, the most rewarding. Part I gives you the mental models to make that leap. In Part II, we'll focus on the exact step-by-step tools to execute your ownership plan once you've taken the plunge.

On 19 February 2019, my last official date at Discovery, I came back from my farewell party at the Discovery office, feeling like a fist had been thrust in my stomach. I was struck by the finality of leaving behind the passionate team of 200 employees and the comfortable, well-lit Discovery office at WeWork in the Bandra Kurla

Complex, Mumbai. From the next day, I'd be working with seven people on rented laptops in the small, cramped living room of my house, stripped of my identity as the head of a major company in India. Did I have it in me to build something meaningful again? What did it take to create a new company from scratch? How much time would it take? Despite reading sixty or seventy books in the months preceding my exit, I couldn't get a clear road map for building a company. Part II gives you that road map. Your actual timings will vary, of course, but you'll go through these rough phases from idea to company:

Table 0.1: WhiteHat Jr phases with month markers

	0	6	12	18	24
MONTHS	"IDEA VALIDATION"	"10X PRODUCT"	"SYSTEM & LOAD TESTING"	"SCALING"	
	PHASE 0	PHASE 1	PHASE 2	PHASE 3	

Source: Created by the author

Month 0—July 2018—is when I first came up with the WhiteHat Jr idea. For the next three months, I didn't incorporate a company until I validated the idea. Post-validation, I incorporated the company and raised our seed funding over the next three months. Then, there were three distinct phases of roughly six months each, from building a product to setting systems and scaling the company to $100 million in revenue. You can use the funding given in Table 0.2 and the revenue as markers of your progress in each phase, knowing, of course, that this is just one trajectory and yours will vary based on your idea and business model.

Table 0.2: WhiteHat Jr funding raised before the start of each phase and the annualized revenue at the end or the last month of the phase

	Phase	Time from Start to End of Phase	Funding (Amount Raised ($Million) at Start of Phase	Annualized Revenue[1] ($Million) at End of Phase
00	'Idea evaluation'	July–November 2018	—	—
11	'10x product'	December 2018–June 2019	Seed: $1.3 million	$2 million
22	'System set up and load testing'	July 2019–February 2020	Series A: $10 million	$12 million
33	'Scaling'	March–August 2020	—[2]	Over $100 million

Notes: [1]*Annualized revenue calculated as monthly booking revenue multiplied by twelve. Example: Phase 1 annualized bookings revenue is July* 2019 *monthly booking revenue multiplied by 12.*

[2]*Series B funding planned at $50 million but turned midway into BYJU's acquisition. We scaled to over $100 million without funding since we had a positive cash flow.*

Source: Created by the author

Within each phase, I've elaborated on areas which entrepreneurs wrestle with the most and can't find easy answers to. I've focused most on the validation and 10x product phase, where you're at the edges of user consciousness and your progress is slow and hard, making you want to give up often. Following the 10x product phase, a company gathers its own momentum as it moves closer from the edges to the centre of users' lives.

Phase 0: Idea Validation

- Start-up Starter Kit Number 1: How to Find Your Game-Changing Ownership Idea
- Start-up Starter Kit Number 2: How to Raise Funding with No Product
- Start-up Starter Kit Number 3: How to Write a Successful Pitch Deck
- Start-up Starter Kit Number 4: How Are Companies Valued?

Phase 1: 10x Product

- Start-up Starter Kit Number 5: How to Start Up with No Co-Founder
- Start-up Starter Kit Number 6: How to Find Product-Market Fit Fast

Phases 2 and 3: Systems Set Up and Scaling

- Start-up Starter Kit Number 7: How to Scale a Company: Three Tools That Work

Finally, I've highlighted mistakes I made in each step. You'll make your own mistakes, of course, but I've tried to cover the most dangerous ones to avoid, so that nothing comes between you and your dream.

Let's get started!

Note: In the chapters that follow, you will see some screenshots and PowerPoint decks. Some of these may be difficult to read because of the limitations of print. For the reader's ease, I have also added these on my website: http://www.karanbajaj.com/

8

Phase 0: Idea Validation

Start-up Starter Kit Number 1

How to Find Your Game-Changing Ownership Idea

Do you want to start your ownership journey but either don't have an idea yet or don't know if the idea is big enough to become a company? In this section, you'll learn a simple framework to generate multiple ownership ideas from scratch and select one that has the potential to impact millions.

First, here are the start-up ideas I considered and evaluated before zeroing in on WhiteHat Jr:

- Idea No. 1: Healthcare Genomics/AI Diagnostic: Collect large sets of Indian gene and disease data and apply artificial intelligence (AI) models to predictively diagnose healthcare issues for similar gene types and create preventive plans.

- Idea No. 2: Farm-to-Table Tech: Enable urban consumers to directly access rural farmers' produce by eliminating supply-chain inefficiencies.
- Idea No. 3: Natural Foods Membership Service: Create one monthly membership service that delivers quality organic, natural products at home under 'food and personal care' categories.
- Idea No. 4: Live Online Coding Classes for Kids (eventually WhiteHat Jr): Enable every kid to be a creator in this world with a creative, activity-based curriculum and 1:1 individualized attention from a teacher.

How do you generate new ideas so that you have plenty of options to evaluate? And how do you pick the one? This three-step approach will work for you in every category:

- **Step 1: Selective 'Power Reading'**
- **Step 2: Founder—Product Fit**
- **Step 3: Evaluation—Internal and External**

Let's dive into each step below:

Step 1: Selective 'Power Reading'

I felt increasingly irrelevant in my late thirties, working in legacy companies right in the middle of the tech revolution. Twenty-one-year-old coders in their garage were releasing products within days that took us years to conceptualize. I became obsessed with learning technology; and over a three-month period in 2018, just before I started WhiteHat

Jr, I read more than seventy books and a few selected blogs to get myself fully immersed in start-ups and technology trends. The books and readings below had the most impact on me:

Books

- ***Zero to One: Notes on Startups, or How to Build the Future*** (2014) by Peter Thiel, with Blake Masters: I was deeply influenced by an idea from the book that the best start-ups are monopolies, either creating new categories, such as AirBnB, or creating products that are ten times superior to the competition, such as Google. As a result, the ideas I conceptualized in the generation phase were new categories in India, and not just marginally superior alternatives to existing products.
- ***The Lean Startup: How Today's Entrepreneurs Use Continuous Innovation to Create Radically Successful Businesses*** (2011) by Eric Ries: I shortlisted ideas that I could prototype and launch quickly, mainly due to this book's research on how successful start-ups launch quickly and co-create the product rapidly with user feedback, as against building products for months in a silo. I found the WhiteHat Jr idea attractive, for instance, because I was able to conceptualize a demo version with no code—create an engaging curriculum, train sample teachers and connect teachers to students over Zoom to deliver it.
- ***Hooked: How to Build Habit-Forming Products*** (2013) by Nir Eyal: The book's core philosophy that all actions on a technology platform should trigger rewards

helped me generate ideas that would be habit-forming for users, for example, Farm-to-Table Tech. Once a user ordered directly from a farm with one click, they would replicate the action daily.

- ***Hacking Growth: How Today's Fastest-Growing Companies Drive Breakout Success*** (2017) by Sean Ellis and Morgan Brown: Start-ups need to do just two things—build well and sell. After reading this book, I brainstormed ideas that would have word-of-mouth built into them so that users would multiply without costs of acquisition multiplying. With the healthcare genomics and AI diagnostic, for instance, I could envision people telling their extended families about it since people cared about their family's health and well-being, first and foremost.
- ***High Output Management*** (1983) by Andy Grover: Your single-most important lever to multiply your output is to inspire and train your team members to deliver the same or more output than you can on your own. Andy Grover, Intel's legendary CEO, has specific, actionable advice on creating great teams and rigorous operations, much of which helped me at the ideation stage itself. I shortlisted the natural foods membership service, for instance, since I knew I'd be able to attract strong talent from companies like Flipkart, which had developed great expertise in online retail.
- ***Measure What Matters: OKRs: The Simple Idea That Drives Ten Times Growth*** (2017) by John Doerr: I set strong metrics for success, even at the ideation stage, thanks to the book. Once I took the WhiteHat Jr idea to prototype, for example, I defined clear objectives and

key results (OKRs) to decide whether it could become a company. I'd set the objective of doing sixty free trials and achieving quantifiable results of ten customers converting to paying users and reporting a Net Promoter Score (NPS) of more than thirty, a benchmark for a good product, before incorporating a company.

- ***The Hard Thing about Hard Things*** (2014) by Ben Horowitz: The book narrates an entrepreneur's no-filters personal journey and gave me a good mental frame on how hard entrepreneurship would be. As a result, I took the discouraging reactions of friends and family, when I told them I was starting up, in my stride, knowing that disapproval and rejection were necessary parts of the journey.

News

- I read actively about newly minted Chinese unicorns to understand what problems they were solving in a market with similar aspirations for upward mobility. Education and health and wellness were recurring themes, and I zeroed in on these.

Blogs

- 'Masters of Scale' with Reid Hoffman: Reid Hoffman, the founder of LinkedIn, interviews world-renowned founders in this blog, and their deep, thoughtful responses became a North Star for me to create and scale a company. I was particularly moved by AirBnB founder Brian Chesky's interview on how they always conceptualized a seven-star experience for their user versus a five-star experience and did their best to deliver that as much as business model costs allowed. From small details like AirBnB hosts putting coffee and toast in the kitchen for guests to large moves like a blanket $1 million insurance for the host's home, the seven-star philosophy made AirBnB a special company; and I tried my hardest to replicate the seven-star thinking in the early days of fleshing out each of the ideas.

- Paul Graham's Blog: From 'The Eighteen Mistakes That Kill Startups' to 'Ideas for Startups', Paul Graham's blog gave me very useful frameworks to identify and evaluate start-up ideas that would endure.

I read widely for a concentrated burst of three months and made a list of the four ideas on page 126-27 that I instinctually thought would work as tech start-ups. What are you 'power reading' about technology in your vertical? This will become your doorway for ownership.

Step 2: Personal Fit Iteration

Next, I checked these ideas for personal fit against just one criterion—flow. Could I see myself fully immersed in the idea and make it my life for seven years, the average time it takes a successful start-up to go from initiation to exit? Mihaly Csikszentmihalyi, a Hungarian-American psychologist, defines flow as those peak, transcendental human experiences where you're so absorbed in an activity that nothing else seems to matter.

High-performing athletes, musicians and artists reported experiencing peak performance levels when work simply 'flowed' out of them without effort, and Mihaly Csikszentmihalyi identified eight characteristics of a flow experience:

1. Complete concentration on the task.
2. Clarity of goals and reward in mind and immediate feedback.
3. Transformation of time (speeding up/slowing down).
4. Effortlessness and ease.
5. Merger of actions and awareness, loss of self-conscious rumination.
6. Feeling of control over the task.
7. Intrinsically rewarding experience.
8. Balance between challenge and skills.

With strong will, I could make any task meet most of the characteristics above, just like I'd done with writing fiction or my job as head of Discovery, but success in entrepreneurship is akin to success in an Olympic event. You must be a perfect fit for the sport. Being good enough just won't cut it. I focused on the two characteristics listed below that I had to feel from deep inside me and couldn't just manufacture with determination:

Intrinsically Rewarding Experience

Are you so deeply interested in and pulled towards your idea that the external rewards don't matter as much as the activity itself? I rejected Idea No. 2, Farm-to-Table Tech, using this criterion. I'd spent some of my childhood years on my grandfather's farm in the Himalayas, so I had an instinctive knowledge of farming, but I'd become urbanized over the years. My heart didn't lift up at the idea of working 10x10x6 (*Founder's typical work-time: 10 a.m.–10 p.m., six days/week*) for seven years to revolutionize the agriculture supply chain in India.

Balance between Challenge and Skills

The flow state is just right, neither too easy nor too hard. Do your unique skills make the challenge of a start-up inviting or intimidating? I eliminated Idea No. 1, Healthcare Genomics/AI, from my list of ideas because I knew nothing about either AI or Indian healthcare. The challenge of understanding two new fields while building a real business was interesting but I knew I'd be overwhelmed in execution.

In contrast, I found both intrinsic passion and the perfect balance of challenge and skills in the WhiteHat Jr 'Kids as creators for life'. School curriculum was unchanged for twenty years, with limited emphasis on critical thinking and creativity. I was deeply passionate about kids becoming builders for life in a world where routine mechanized tasks would be done by a machine. My brand-building experience in Procter & Gamble and Kraft made me a great fit for building a new category from scratch. And even though education and technology were both new fields for me, I knew I would learn them by seeing the product from my own kids' eyes.

Step 3: Evaluation—Internal and External

Finally, I quickly evaluated the ideas for broad appeal using these two approaches:

Internal Evaluation: The 'Magnitude and Depth' Formula

- **Magnitude: Does your idea touch millions of users?**
- **Depth: Does it meet a deep, fundamental human need ten times better than the alternative?**

I eliminated Idea No. 3, Natural Foods Membership Service, using this evaluation. Access to natural, healthy food was a deep, fundamental human need, but was it truly unmet for millions of users around the world? People who were health-conscious had figured out healthy products, and any alternative I would create would be more convenient but not ten times better.

The WhiteHat Jr idea, in contrast, had the potential to touch millions of kids around the world and create a ten times better alternative to the unorganized creative/critical thinking hobby space for kids.

External Evaluation: Test for Actual Market Appeal by Building a Low-Code Prototype Immediately.

I created WhiteHat Jr's first website in seven days with an Upwork designer. In parallel, I created the first version of a six-class coding curriculum using Zoom and Scratch, with a local science teacher in Mumbai. Then I posted about the classes on my personal Facebook page.

Figure 8.1: WhiteHat Jr's first prototype

Source: Provided by the author

Figure 8.2: First prototype development time and investment

• Development Time: 14 Days
• Full-time Employees: 0
• Total Investment: <Rs 1 Lakh

Source: Created by the author

Sixty users signed up for a free trial class from Facebook. I called each user myself after the class. Parents told us that kids had loved the class but as parents, they didn't know what to make of coding classes since it wasn't a part of school curriculum. I explained to parents the beauty and benefit of kids creating things in the world. Most cut my call in the middle, but twelve among sixty parents resonated with the idea of a kid being a builder for life and bought a six-class package.

I knew then that we could create a global category. We'd got our first paying users cold, rather through personal connections. They had understood the category on its own merits. Now, we had to replicate this process on a large scale. A free trial was frictionless and millions of users would sign up for it. We just had to deliver a great product and set up a sales organization that communicated the same passion I had about the category to users after the free trial; and one day, we would make coding a global category.

How to Get Your Game-Changing Ownership Idea: A Summary

Follow this step-by-step framework to identify and evaluate your ownership idea. Keep searching, keep iterating, keep evaluating, until all your boxes are checked as shown below in Table 8.1.

Table 8.1: Idea evaluation matrix

	Idea	Selective Reading	Personal Fit—Passion	Personal Fit—Complexity	Internal Evaluation—Scale	External Evaluation—Test
11	Farm-to-Table Tech	✓	✗			
22	Healthcare AI/Genomics	✓	✓	✗		
33	Natural Foods Membership	✓	✓	✓	✗	
44	WhiteHat Jr Live Online Creativity for Kids	✓	✓	✓	✓	✓

Source: Created by the author

My Mistake

As a non-tech founder, I should have read more domain-specific books and blogs on product management and design during my power-reading phase and not just about start-ups and technology. Once you start up, the wheel runs so fast that you have little time to step away from it. Given my lack of understanding of the product role, I hired the first product leader in the company only a year after starting up when we had crossed 200 employees and $5 million in annualized revenue. I was the sole product manager until then.

During this time, I haphazardly attacked various elements of the user journey, overemphasizing on kids' class experience and under-weighting parents' post-class operations. As a result, our product experience was patchy for a year. We were fortunate to create a category with no alternatives, so users forgave our mistakes, or else they would've shifted to more sophisticated competitors. Later, I understood that product management was core across the whole company and restructured the product function to hire dedicated leaders for:

- **Growth:** Daily experiments to reduce the marketing acquisitions costs, for example, referral programmes and trial registration journey simplification.
- **Experience**: Improving kids' learning experience by initiatives such as giving them emojis and stars when they did well in class and building a gamification engine to make post-class projects and worksheets joyful.
- **Delivery:** Strengthening our product delivery for parents by constant improvement in teacher quality with real-time report cards on their performance and operational improvements to allow one-click rescheduling.

Three months after the key roles were filled, we created an elegant product with a very strong NPS of 67 against the earlier NPS of 50. Without the dedicated product focus, we would not perhaps have survived the competitive onslaught in the category when the bigger players launched their copycat coding products on seeing our early traction.

Your Learnings

Read books and blogs widely to fill your knowledge gaps during the power-reading phase, focusing both on:

- General start-up knowledge, such as *Zero to One, The Lean Startup,* and *The Hard Thing About Hard Things.*
- Domain-specific knowledge on product, tech, design and operations, such as *Hooked, Hacking Growth* and *High Output Management*.

9

Phase 0: Idea Validation

Start-up Starter Kit Number 2

How to Raise Funding with No Product

My third novel, *The Seeker*, was rejected sixty-one times in the US. Eventually, after thirty months of nearly daily revisions, Penguin Random House published it worldwide. Three years of life gone in publishing a novel!

I found the start-up fundraising process much saner, in comparison.

It took sixty days from idea to securing Rs 10 crore ($1.3 million) seed funding for WhiteHat Jr. And this was in late 2018, well before the incredible funding momentum we're seeing now in India.

What a golden time to be an entrepreneur. Now that you have your ownership idea, here's how to go from idea to secured funding in rapid timing.

Step 1: Create a Low Fidelity Prototype (14 Days)

I spoke to a friend the day I had come up with the WhiteHat Jr idea, one month after giving my notice to Discovery, while still serving my six-month notice period.

He said it was too small.

Coincidentally, I had a meeting with a large tech company CEO the next day for a project for Discovery, who I was convinced would 'get it'. The CEO said that coding for kids was years ahead of its time in India and it would never work.

So, I did what I should've done the moment the idea had come to me.

I took it to the users.

Start-ups always lie at the edges of systems, not at the centre of them. So, people's opinions, even experts', are seldom useful. Instead of expert validation, seek user validation by taking your idea to prototype immediately.

How to Build a Low Fidelity/Zero-Code Prototype in Thirty Days with Minimal Spend?

A. Create a website sketch based on the essence of your idea in seven days.
B. Brief a website designer and front-end developer on Upwork, the freelance platform, to make the website live in seven days.
C. In parallel, create the simplest version of your product for users. For WhiteHat Jr, I contacted a teacher who ran her own science classes in our neighbourhood and created the first version of a six-class coding curriculum

with her open-source tools such as Zoom and Scratch in fourteen days.

You're ready for your Beta!

Your actual timing will vary based on your product. But I would argue that the simplest version of your product, often a zero-code solution, will take a fraction of the time and resources you think it will. For instance, even a seemingly complex idea like Farm-to-Table Tech can be prototyped without tech by arranging for sixty users to receive a farm's produce directly at their home for one week for free. After the trial, you can attempt to sell them a daily subscription of farm vegetables at a lower price than what they get in the market to check the commercial appeal of the idea. Similarly, you can determine any idea's potential in a short time frame and with limited investment if you cut off all the superfluous stuff.

'The sculpture is already complete within the marble block, before I start my work. It is already there, I just have to chisel away the superfluous material.' —Michaelangelo

Step 2: Get Your First Paying Customers to Create a Category (Fourteen Days)

With the website live, I posted about free trial coding classes for kids on my personal Facebook page. We filled up our limit of sixty students and manually scheduled trial classes with the science teacher (who later became my very valued first employee). Soon after, we had our first paying customer. The customer paid the teacher the old-fashioned way—with a bank transfer (see Figure 9.1).

Figure 9.1: WhiteHat Jr's first paying customer email

Tue. Jun 19, 2018, 10:30 AM

to Gauri, Karan, Gauri

Hi Gauri,

I'm happy to go ahead.

[redacted] is going to school currently and hence available only between 4pm and 7pm UK time on weekdays and 10:30-4pm on weekends. He is available all days till 5th July except Mondays and 29th June.

Let me know what time works with you.

I'll transfer the money to your account today. It should be in your account by late tomorrow.

Can you also let me know what will I need to do after [redacted] has finished his class. How can I keep his interest alive and keep him going really?

Regards,

Source: Provided by the author

Soon after, twelve out of sixty trial customers agreed to pay after my sales calls. I had a strong intuition then that we could create a global category. We just had to replicate the process of finding the first twelve customers at scale. Today, WhiteHat Jr operates as BYJU's FutureSchool in six countries—India, the US, the UK, Australia, Brazil and Mexico—and five categories—maths, coding, music, arts and English—with millions of users. But the basic framework of advertising for a trial class, an engaging trial class with a live teacher and a creation-oriented curriculum that kids love has stuck.

If you have just a handful of paying customers, you can perhaps create a global category with millions of users. Just scale what worked for those initial users. That's all you need to move confidently to the next step.

Step 3: Reach Out Cold to Venture Capitalists and Close the Deal! (Thirty Days)

We grew the pilot to thirty paying customers over two weeks. Then, I made a list of India's top thirty venture capitalists and approached them completely cold on LinkedIn, as below (Figure 9.2):

Figure 9.2: LinkedIn cold outreach

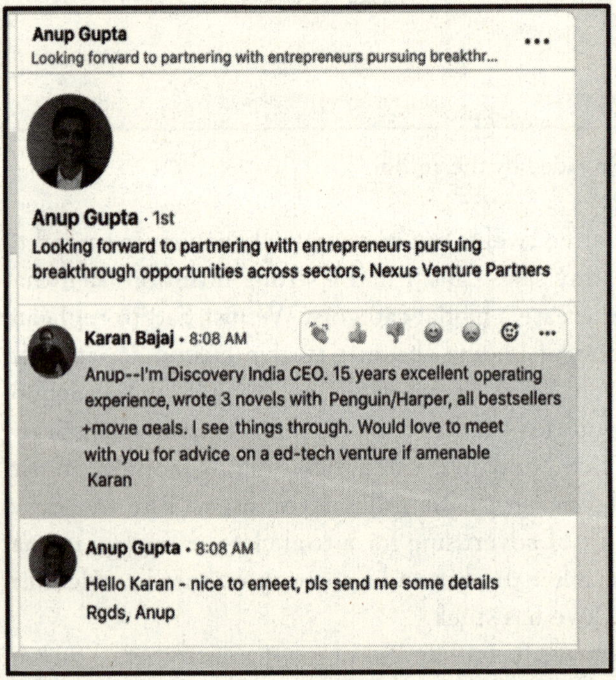

Source: Provided by the author

My experiences with venture capitalists were a mixed bag. Some replied, most didn't. Among the ones who replied, many went cold in the middle of the evaluation process. I wish venture capitalists understood these five characteristics that every early-stage entrepreneur looks for during fundraising:

Incredibly Fast Response Time

I was building the team and product from my own savings after the prototype, and I knew I would run out soon without external funding. Time is your enemy as an entrepreneur and fast response is perhaps the number one desired venture capitalist trait.

For instance, Omidyar's head Roopa Kudva responded within hours to my outreach despite being out of office (see Figure 9.3).

Figure 9.3: Omidyar cold outreach response

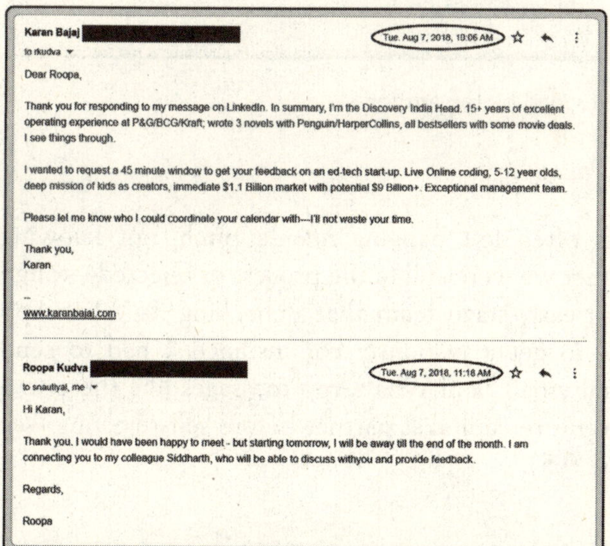

Karan Bajaj Tue. Aug 7, 2018, 10:06 AM

to rkudva

Dear Roopa,

Thank you for responding to my message on LinkedIn. In summary, I'm the Discovery India Head. 15+ years of excellent operating experience at P&G/BCG/Kraft; wrote 3 novels with Penguin/HarperCollins, all bestsellers with some movie deals. I see things through.

I wanted to request a 45 minute window to get your feedback on an ed-tech start-up. Live Online coding, 5-12 year olds, deep mission of kids as creators, immediate $1.1 Billion market with potential $9 Billion+. Exceptional management team.

Please let me know who I could coordinate your calendar with—I'll not waste your time.

Thank you,
Karan

--
www.karanbajaj.com

Roopa Kudva Tue. Aug 7, 2018, 11:18 AM

to snautiyal, me

Hi Karan,

Thank you. I would have been happy to meet - but starting tomorrow, I will be away till the end of the month. I am connecting you to my colleague Siddharth, who will be able to discuss withyou and provide feedback.

Regards,

Roopa

Source: Provided by the author

First Conviction

In all my funding rounds, I saw that the moment you had the first investor term sheet, suddenly everyone else followed. The best venture capitalists show independent conviction rather than waiting for others to jump first. For instance, Anup Gupta from Nexus was the first to show conviction when others were still indecisive (see Figure 9.4).

Figure 9.4: Nexus investment confirmation message

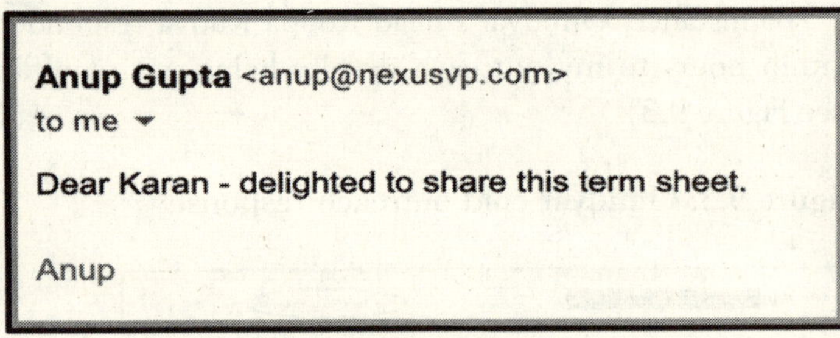

Anup Gupta <anup@nexusvp.com>
to me

Dear Karan - delighted to share this term sheet.

Anup

Source: Provided by the author

Closure Follow-up

4. I was often left hanging *after* a pitch, not knowing whether we were still in the process or rejected—tough for an early-stage team that's checking its WhatsApp 24×7 to get a response. For instance, I had to send several emails and WhatsApp messages like these to a top venture capitalist partner before self-rejecting (see Figure 9.5).

Figure 9.5: Sample follow-up after pitch

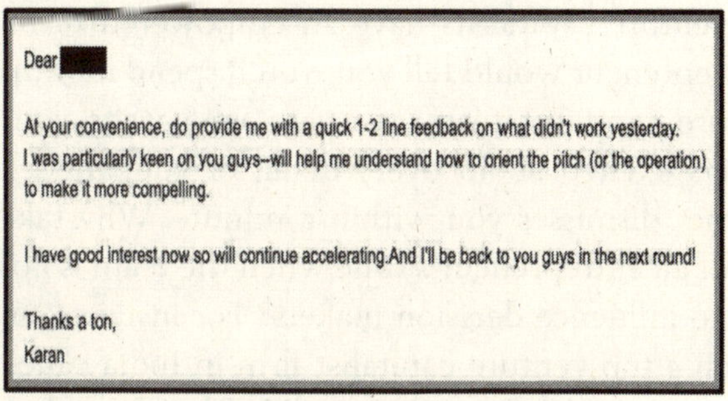

Dear [redacted]

At your convenience, do provide me with a quick 1-2 line feedback on what didn't work yesterday.
I was particularly keen on you guys--will help me understand how to orient the pitch (or the operation) to make it more compelling.

I have good interest now so will continue accelerating.And I'll be back to you guys in the next round!

Thanks a ton,
Karan

Source: Provided by the author

Entrepreneur Respect

I was made to wait four hours in the Bengaluru office of a top venture capitalist, after which she dismissed the presentation within seven minutes. My pitch should've been better, for sure, but investor rejections, too, can be dignified and respectful. For instance, this top venture capitalist's polite and dignified rejection, thanks to Ravi Kaushik, WaterBridge Ventures (see Figure 9.6).

Figure 9.6: Positive investor rejection message

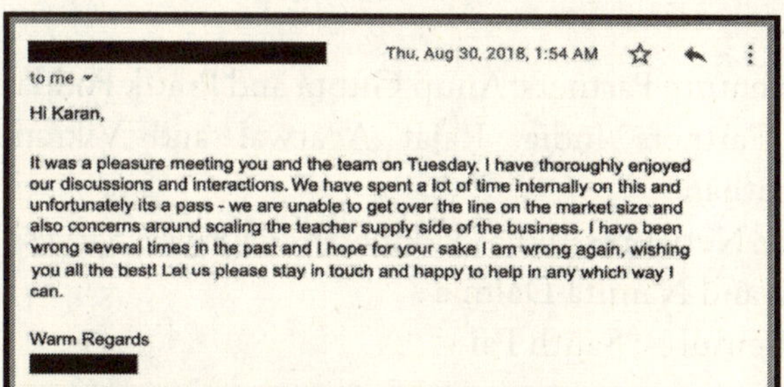

Thu, Aug 30, 2018, 1:54 AM

to me

Hi Karan,

It was a pleasure meeting you and the team on Tuesday. I have thoroughly enjoyed our discussions and interactions. We have spent a lot of time internally on this and unfortunately its a pass - we are unable to get over the line on the market size and also concerns around scaling the teacher supply side of the business. I have been wrong several times in the past and I hope for your sake I am wrong again, wishing you all the best! Let us please stay in touch and happy to help in any which way I can.

Warm Regards

Source: Provided by the author

Empowered Team

Finally, top venture capitalists have an empowered team. As every entrepreneur would tell you, you'll spend months with a venture capitalist team associate who visits your office and gets excited about every detail of your model, but the partner dismisses you within a minute. Why take up so much of an entrepreneur's time when the team is not empowered to influence decision makers? For instance, an associate from a top venture capitalist firm in India called me to meet him at the Four Seasons Hotel in Mumbai, an hour-long commute from Andheri East where our first office was, twice in two weeks. Next, he asked me to fly down to meet him in Delhi on my own expense. Then, he introduced me to one of the firm's partners over email. I met the partner on my second visit to Delhi, again at my own expense, who rejected me within a few minutes based on his 'instinct'. The associate could've just told the partner about the company after the first visit itself, saving me eight weeks of time and two flight trips worth of money.

Among the top thirty Indian venture capitalists I reached out to, the ones listed below exceeded my expectations on all five criteria detailed above even though three firms—Matrix, Blume and Sequoia—rejected my pitch:

1. Nexus Venture Partners: Anup Gupta and Pratik Poddar
2. Matrix Partners India: Rajat Agarwal and Vikram Vaidyanathan
3. Omidyar Networks India: Siddharth Nautiyal, Sarvesh Kanodia and Namita Dalmia
4. Blume Ventures: Sajith Pai

5. Sequoia India: Abheek Anand, Rajan Anandan and Ravishankar GV

Within a month of pitching, I had my first term sheet. Easier than getting a novel published! But unlike a novel where a book deal is almost the end of the laborious process, getting a funding deal is barely the start of building a company. I don't remember celebrating either my seed or Series A funding rounds for even a day; there was always so much more to get done. And funding was just a small milestone indicating the next stage rather than a destination of any consequence. But early funding did make the journey later less hard, so I hope this is useful for aspiring entrepreneurs debating whether to take a plunge.

My Mistake

Sequoia, Matrix and Blume did their homework on me, collecting blind references from my ex-colleagues from Discovery and Procter & Gamble in India, and even my IIM batchmates from two decades ago. Everyone swore by my relentless work ethic. The firms wanted to invest in me but eventually held back for one reason: the coding market size appeared too small in India. How many people would pay to make their kids creators in India when they struggled to make both ends meet?

Out of 280 million households in India, only 45 million earn more than Rs 10 lakh per annum. Most of the Indian Internet industry, from e-commerce to food delivery, rely on these users to make their start-ups financially successful (see Table 9.1).[1]

Table 9.1: Indian household categorization by income

Household Categorization	Average Annual Household Income (Rs)	Number of Households (Million)
India-1	30 lakh	23
India-2	10 lakh	22
India-Mass (India-3)	4 lakh	235

Source: Sajith Pai blog, https://sajithpai.com/

For a category like K12 education, your target households narrow further to those with kids in the age group of 6–18 years, making it a 23 million[2] household market. Further, venture capitalists suspected that despite my best efforts, I wouldn't be able to convince households even in India-2 to embrace coding or creativity, given their focus on IIT and other competitive examinations, reducing the perceived market to just above 10 million households. They rejected investing in such a niche market.

I should've demonstrated a bigger target market.

Despite no Indian education company having succeeded in penetrating the US, I had firm conviction based on my travels that we could target a global market. However, I hesitated to present my international launch plan in my first pitch for fear of appearing impractical when I had all of thirty Indian paying customers in the prototype.

In retrospect, I should've tested in the US and demonstrated early interest among users there to present a global vision. Similarly, I could have created a sharper thesis on why mass India would embrace coding.

Your Learnings

You'll perhaps be asked a question on market size when you present your new-to-the-world idea to venture capitalists. Solve it by:

Targeting an International Market

I learnt from my mistake and ran a test among 100 users in the US for our Series A funding round. As expected, kids in the US loved the product as much as kids in India did. Creation was a deep, fundamental human need with no geographical barriers. Now, I presented a 10x market size, from 10 million households to 100 million households, by showing the seven markets we would target among the top ten largest markets in the world (see Table 9.2).

Table 9.2: Country market potential analyses

Country	Households (Million)	Households with Children[3] (per cent)	Paying Capacity (per cent)	Target Households	Language	Execution Ease[4]
China	523	57	15	44.7	Chinese	Low
India	280	63	15	26.5	English	High
United States	132	29	60	23.1	English	High
Indonesia	69	67	15	7.0	Bahsa	Medium
Brazil	64	47	15	4.5	Portuguese	Medium
Russia	56	25	60	8.5	Russian	Low
Japan	55	25	60	8.4	Japanese	Low
Nigeria	42	68	15	4.3	English	High
Germany	40	18	60	4.4	German + English	Medium
Bangladesh	38	77	15	4.4	English	High
Mexico	34	54	15	2.8	Spanish	Medium

Country	Households (Million)	Households with Children[3] (per cent)	Paying Capacity (per cent)	Target Households	Language	Execution Ease[4]
Pakistan	32	81	15	3.9	English	Low
France	30	25	60	4.5	French	Medium
United Kingdom	30	27	60	4.8	English	High
Philippines	26	70	15	2.7	English	Medium
Vietnam	26	58	15	2.2	Vietnamese/ English	Medium
Italy	25	23	60	3.5	Italian	Medium
Others (South Africa, Canada, Australia)	42		15 for South Africa, 60 for Canada and Australia	5.6	English	High
		Total (High + Medium)		100.3		

Source: Created by the author

Creating a 'Delight Don't Dilute' Strategy for India's Depth

How do you reach India mass, the next 235 million households in India?

Procter & Gamble pioneered a strategy called 'Delight Don't Dilute' for mass entry. Rather than just labelling lower-income users as price-conscious and offering a lesser version of your product at a lower price, start with the user's unique needs in mind. What would truly delight then, given the context of their life? Consumer goods companies used this approach to launch laundry detergent sachets.[5] Rather than a small sachet being just a randomly sized, low-price version of their core 1 kilogram detergent bag, they researched and designed the sachet to have just enough detergent—25 grams—for rural consumers to wash their special clothes, like kids' uniforms and office clothes, once a week.

Users were delighted and within just a couple of years, the Indian sachet market became bigger than the decades-old bag market due to the sheer volume of users in mass India.

Our first instinct to win the mass India consumer was to create a mobile phone coding course for them. But we knew we wouldn't be able to deliver our core delight of a live class with a teacher on a small mobile. Thus, we abandoned the idea. Instead, we chose to 'delight not dilute' by creating a new school model. We partnered with schools in lower-income towns to introduce coding curriculum physically in schools and sourced and trained schoolteachers on coding so that every child in India had the same access to being a creator without barriers of income or infrastructure. I should've presented this vision of reaching the next 235 million households in the pitch stage itself.

Your best defence against venture capitalist rejection is to have a large target market. Increase your market size ten times immediately by thinking global and presenting a custom vision for your product for the next 257 million households in India who deserve the same access to your breakthrough vision as the first 23 million.

10

Start-up Starter Kit Number 3

How to Write a Successful Pitch Deck

YOUR pitch deck should answer, with 100 per cent conviction, the only two questions that truly matter for an investor:

1. How strong is your business today?
2. How big and obvious is your vision for tomorrow?

That's why I recommend only these twelve slides for a pitch deck, structured into a Rule of Four, three sections of four slides each. Just do Section One right, though, and you'll have a high probability of securing funding. Note that this exact layout will also work for subsequent funding rounds (Series A, B, C) as the questions don't change, only the scale gets bigger (see Figure 10.1).

Figure 10.1: Agenda slide

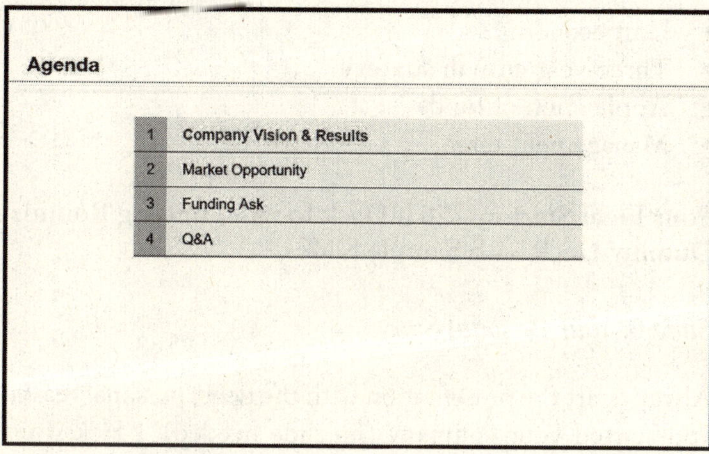

Source: Provided by the author

Section 1: Company Vision and Results

- Your personal story
- Company results: Growth and performance vs plan
- Company vision: Your big and obvious vision
- Category creation strategy: The 'Rule of Three'
- Consumer love: NPS, engagement, testimonials

Section 2: Market Opportunity

- Market size
- Category tailwinds: Why now?
- Your tech disruption in the market
- Competitive differentiation

Section 3: Funding Request

- Unit economics
- Three-year growth strategy
- Application of funds
- Management team

Your Ideal Start-up Pitch Deck for All Funding Rounds: Dummy Deck with Sample Slides

Slide 0: Your Personal Story

Always start the presentation with the deep, personal reason you started your company (no slide needed). I kicked off every presentation, especially in later funding rounds, with my passion for kids to create things early because I discovered the depth and meaning creation brought to my own life very late at the age of twenty-eight, when I wrote my first novel. Research shows that kids peak in creativity at the age of five, followed by a steep decline after, as more rules and systems enter their life. With coding, kids would build their own games, apps and products, getting the confidence that everything in the man-made world is an object created by someone; and they'll build remarkable things too. WhiteHat Jr existed for kids all over the world, starting with my own, to express their natural destiny as creators in this world.

Slide 1: Company Results

Growth and performance versus plan, even if you have thirty customers! Growth today is the best indicator of your potential for tomorrow, so always start with this.

Figure 10.2: Sample first slide of the pitch deck

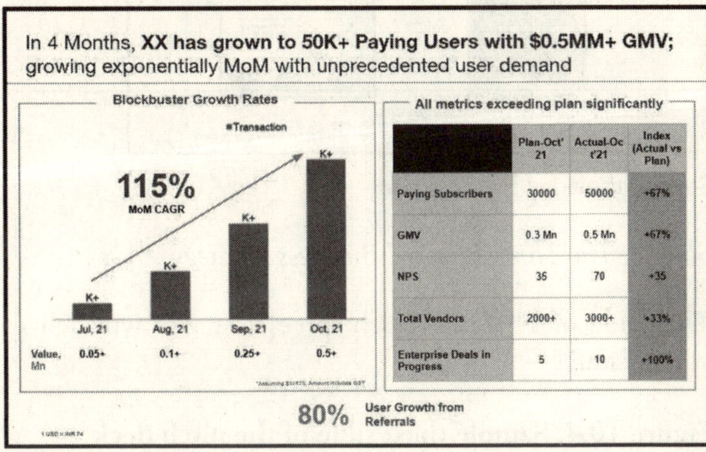

Source: Provided by the author

Slide 2: Company Vision

Your Big and Obvious Vision—how will it impact millions of users or meet a deep human need?

Figure 10.3: Sample second slide of the pitch deck

Source: Provided by the author

Slide 3: The Three-Pronged Business Strategy

The 'Rule of Three'—Which three strategies will deliver your vision?

Figure 10.4: Sample third slide of the pitch deck

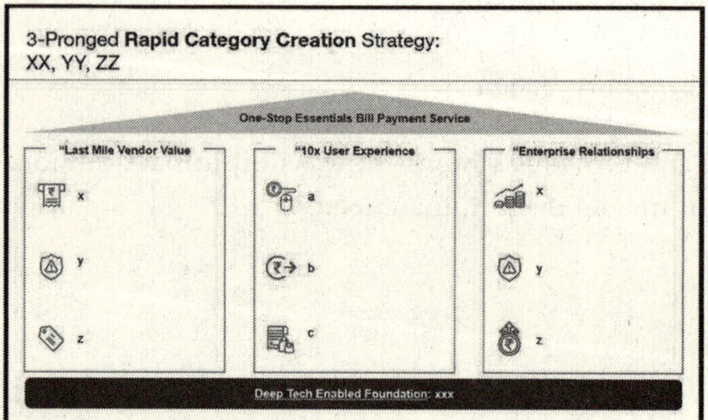

Source: Provided by the author

Slide 4: Consumer Love

NPS, engagement, testimonials—demonstrate how consumers don't just like but *love* your product.

Figure 10.5: Sample fourth slide of the pitch deck

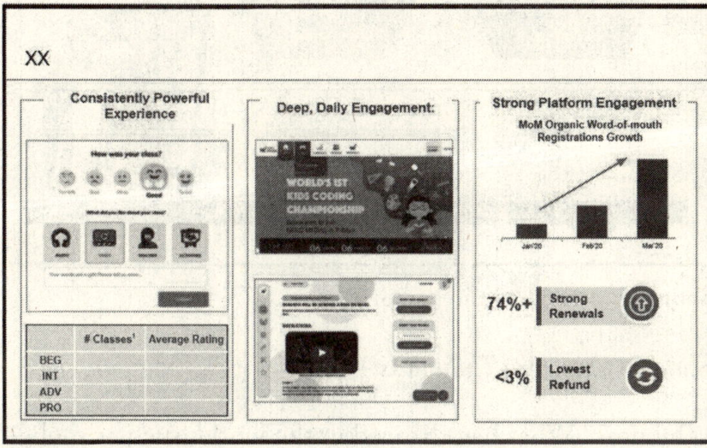

Source: Provided by the author

Slide 5: Market Size

Simple visual calculation showing the number of users multiplied by the average revenue per user, resulting in billions of dollars of market size per power law. You don't need complicated Service Addressable Market (SAM) or Total Addressable Market (TAM) projections.

Figure 10.6: Sample fifth slide of the pitch deck

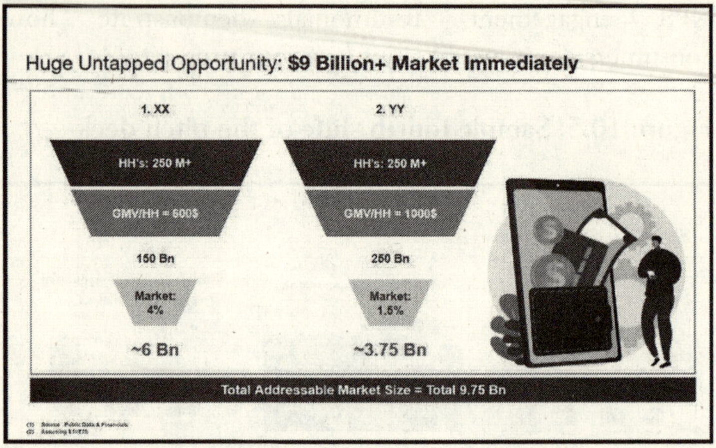

Source: Provided by the author

Slide 6: Category Tailwinds

Why now? What has changed in the world, such as mobile penetration or non-metro adoption, to make your idea more relevant than ever?

Figure 10.7: Sample sixth slide of the pitch deck

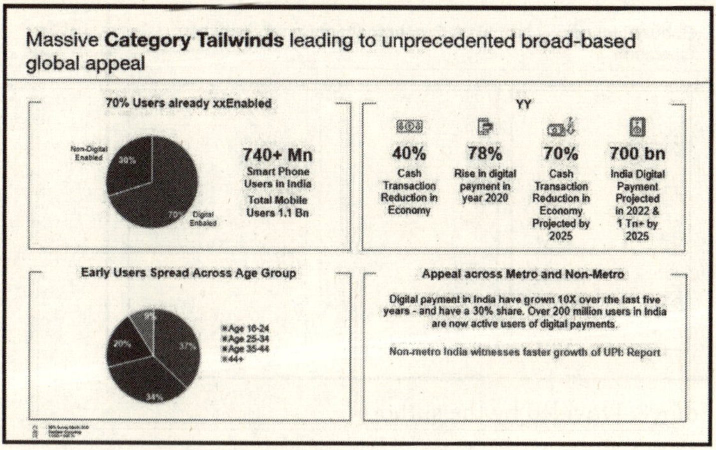

Source: Provided by the author

Slide 7: Your Tech Disruption in the Market

How will your product tech give tenfold user experience?

Figure 10.8: Sample seventh slide of the pitch deck

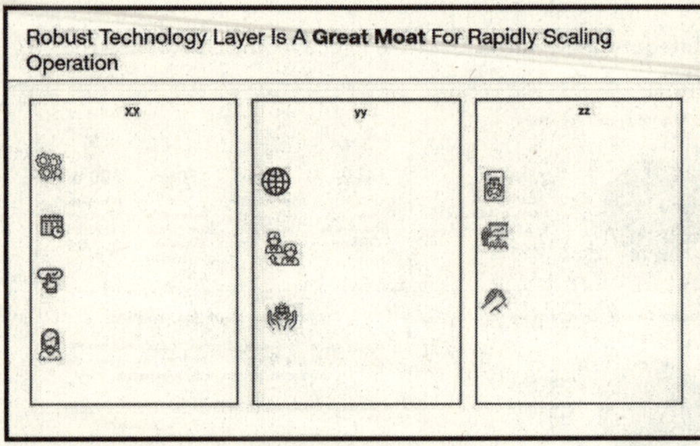

Source: Provided by the author.

Slide 8: Competitive Differentiation

Visually demonstrate why you're in a blue ocean compared to established players

Figure 10.9: Sample eighth slide of the pitch deck

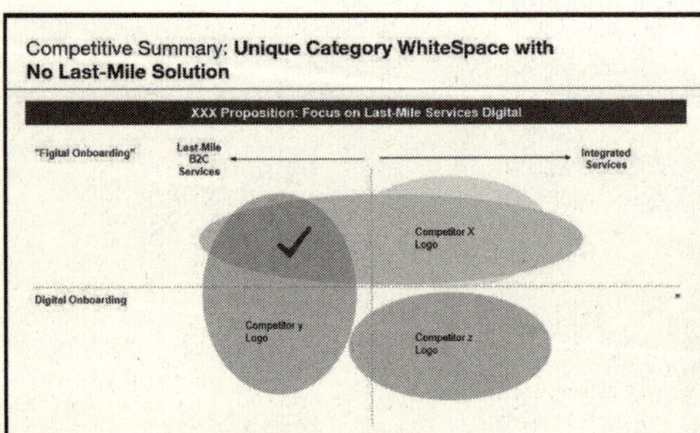

Source: Provided by the author

Slide 9: Unit Economics

Demonstrate strong fiscal discipline delivering positive unit economics.

Figure 10.10: Sample ninth slide of the pitch deck

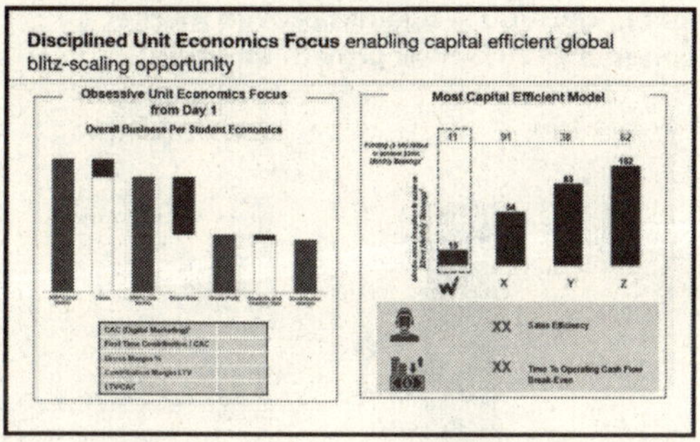

Source: Provided by the author

Slide 10: Three-Year Growth Strategy

Simple charts to show the three-year growth plan which sets up the funding request as below (see Figure 10.11).

Figure 10.11: Sample tenth slide of the pitch deck

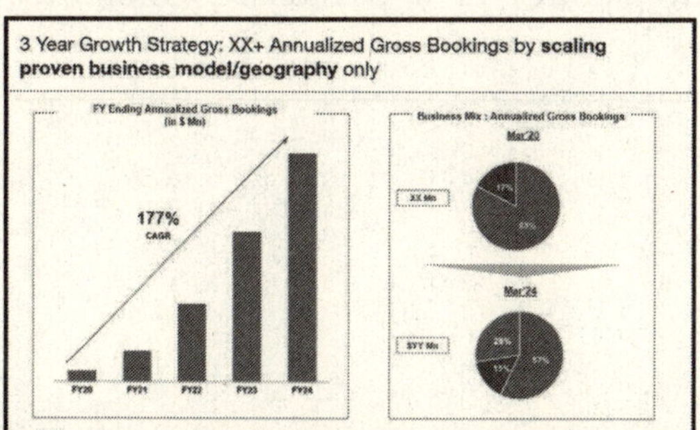

Source: Provided by the author

Slide 11: Application of Funds

Fund deployment buckets based on the above strategy

Figure 10.12: Sample eleventh slide of the pitch deck

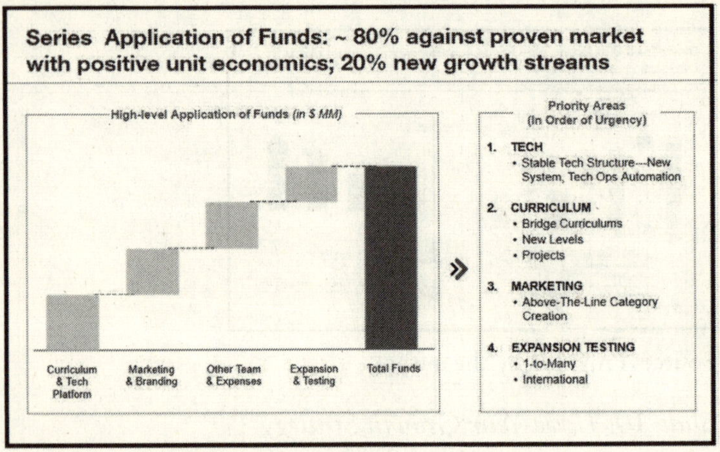

Source: Provided by the author

Slide 12: Management Team

Close strong with pictures of a passionate, committed management team.

Figure 10.13: Sample twelfth slide of the pitch deck

Source: Provided by the author

These twelve slides, done right, will pack enough punch for a top venture capitalist to dive deeper into your model, following which business model strength and your team conviction will win the day.

Bonus: Make the Perfect Funding Deck

Presentation Formatting Expert Freelancer Contact

Venture capitalists spend an average of three minutes and forty-four seconds on a pitch deck.[1] Your funding decks should make a great first impression. I used the Slide Marvels freelance team to make slides look professional, and they make the deck look much more polished than my first attempt—despite my eighteen months of slide creation experience at the Boston Consulting Group.[2]

Financial Models: Legal/Finance Freelance Team Contact

You may find it bewildering, as I did, to build financial models and set up legal entities when you've barely got a product idea. The Treelife team helped me navigate the full journey from seed to acquisition.[3]

My Mistake

I spent two weeks on a detailed theoretical three-year financial model for WhiteHat Jr, hiring an Upwork consultant to help me. We barely touched on financial models in the Investment Committee (IC) meetings of the venture capitalist, beyond a basic check on how the unit economics would be positive. All that investors know financially at this stage is at best estimates.

My financial modelling would have been much more convincing if I had a larger-scale prototype, for example, 1,000 trials in India with multiple teachers instead of the sixty trials I had with one teacher, in order to have an exact estimate of customer acquisition costs (CAC) for both students and teachers, validate our pricing assumptions and show market size depth by attracting both high- and low-income users. Your results today are your best indicators of your vision for tomorrow. I should have delivered more and projected less.

With a broader prototype, I would perhaps not have received twenty rejections out of the top thirty venture capitalists off the gate and been able to close the seed round faster than the three months I took.

Your Learnings

Make your presentation stronger by making your prototype wider. A strong prototype with in-market test results will add substance to all slides in your deck, not just the financial model. For example, if your test attracted a wide demographic of users, you can project a larger market size. Similarly, your competitive advantage is believable if users see a noticeable difference in your product compared to that of well-established players in your space. Your pitch will shine with conviction if you're delivering today what you're projecting for tomorrow.

11

Start-up Starter Kit Number 4
How Are Companies Valued?

WhiteHat Jr was valued at $30 million in our Series A funding round in September 2019.

Nine months later, we received term sheets for up to a valuation of $450 million.

What made the company fifteen times more valuable in just nine months?

Yes, our business expanded. The team got stronger. But there was a deeper change that happened.

Our vision grew.

Start-up valuations are strange at an early stage. A young start-up's value is almost all in the future and not in the present.

How do you mathematically value a dream?

Here I share detailed personal learnings on valuation and ownership, including mistakes I made, which I hope will be useful for folks planning to start their own companies. Also, for those who're often puzzled over why young twenty-month-old start-ups are valued higher than twenty-year-old companies.

First, here is WhiteHat Jr's valuation progression (Table 11.1).

Table 11.1: WhiteHat Jr key valuation dates

Funding Round	Date of Closure	Valuation*
Seed	December 2018	$6 million
Series A	September 2019	$30 million
Series B (Turned midway into acquisition by BYJU's)	July 2020	$300 million**

Notes: *Post-money valuation

**Acquisition cash amount. In parallel, we received Series B Fund-raising Term Sheets: $250–450 million

Source: Provided by the author

My Learnings

The only two things that matter for valuation are: (i) your future vision and (ii) your current business.

Your Future Vision. How 'Big and Obvious' Is Your Vision for Tomorrow?

In 2018, I presented WhiteHat Jr's vision as live coding for kids in India to introduce them to the most important skill of the future (Figure 11.1).

Figure 11.1: WhiteHat Jr's December 2018 seed presentation vision slide: 'Live coding for kids'

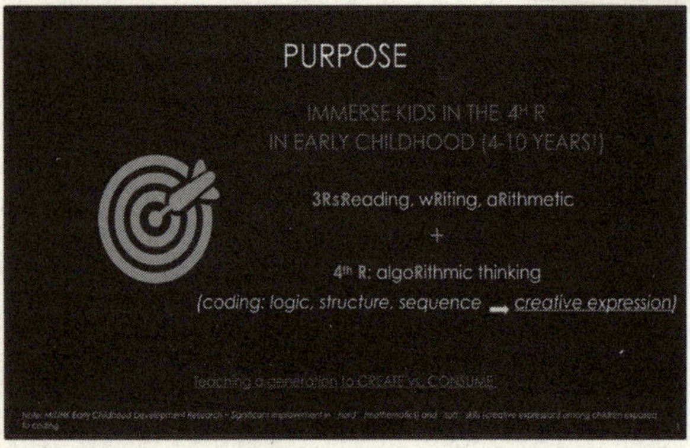

Source: Provided by the author

By 2020, I was confidently stating our real vision of enabling every kid in the world to be a builder and a creator from a consumer (Figure 11.2).

Figure 11.2: WhiteHat Jr's March 2020 Series B presentation vision slide: 'Enabling a generation to create rather than consume'

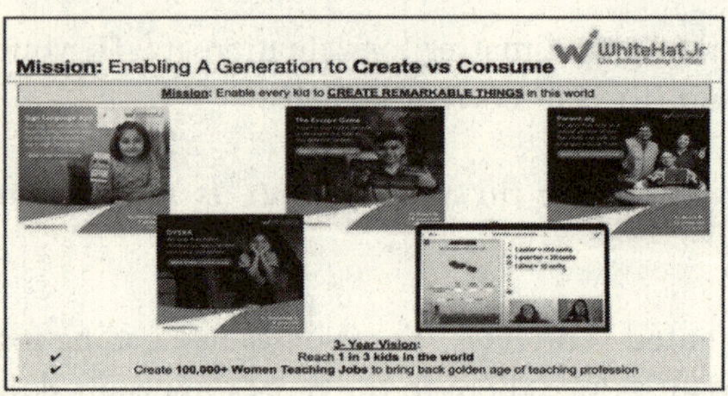

Source: Provided by the author

The 2020 vision was big and obvious, encompassing multiple countries from India to the world, and categories from coding to mathematics, music and arts. Kids would build their own apps in coding, compositions in music, animated films in art and solve real-world problems with mathematics, all assisted by the warmth and encouragement of a dedicated teacher, ushering in a new era of customized, creative learning in the world versus the mass production approach of schools. Every investor wanted to be a part of this vision. Valuation size was almost an afterthought. In contrast, how I presented the vision in 2018 was small and specific.

My thesis was the same in 2018 as it was in 2020, but I was so jaded by the early responses to the idea from friends and family—'no one will pay for creativity in India', and 'no Indian consumer company has succeeded outside India'—that I deliberately underplayed my vision to sound 'practical' enough to secure funding. I thought I would prove myself by solving a narrow problem first, but if I were to do it again, I would have confidently stated the larger vision that led me to create the company in 2018 itself.

I would probably have raised more funding at a higher valuation with a bigger vision in 2018.

Do you have a big vision to transform the world? Yes, it may start with a small, specific step, but don't hesitate to paint your full vision. The larger your ambitions, the larger will be your company's projected future value.

Your Current Business: How Real Is Your Business Today?

I started all my funding decks with a business growth chart (see Figure 11.3).

Figure 11.3: June 2020: First slide of WHJ pitch deck

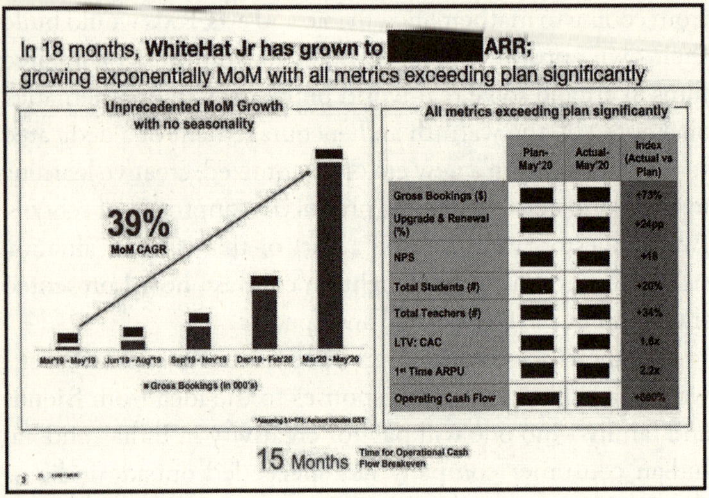

Source: Provided by the author.

Business growth *today* is the best validation of your vision for *tomorrow*. Users are trading an asset they deeply value—their money—for your vision so that it has real value for them. Or else they still don't share your dream for a better world.

All the other elements—your team, technology, intellectual property (IP), competitive multiples—that feed into valuation calculations are inputs into the vision and the business growth. For example, a big vision typically attracts great people; great people come together to make great IP; and great IP means you break all competitive benchmarks.

Start-ups are hard but the good news is you just need to focus on two things: your visionary product and your business. And almost nothing else. Founder's personal brand building, investor coffee meetings, networking events, celebratory social media posts, PR articles, industry conferences—all these are useless for driving value.

You just need to build and sell. And the rest just follows.

WhiteHat Jr's Eighteen-Month Seed-to-Acquisition Journey: Other Learnings on Valuation and Ownership

I wish I'd seen a chart like the one below earlier (Table11.2), especially in the seed stage, when I didn't know how to value my idea since it was little more than a PowerPoint presentation. Nor did I know how much ownership to dilute to raise capital.

Table 11.2: 2018–20: WhiteHat Jr ownership chart

Funding Round	Funding Raised (million)	Valuation (million)[1]	Founder Ownership (per cent)	Investor Ownership (per cent)	ESOP–Employee Ownership
Seed: December 2018	$1.3	$6	60	21	19
Series A: September 2019	$10	$30	39	47	14
Acquisition: Cash Exit: July 2020	-	$300	39	47	14

Source: Created by the author

A Few Quick Observations

- Seed-stage valuations are pretty much pointless, but cash is useful: WhiteHat Jr's destiny would be completely unimpacted by a valuation lower or higher than the $6 million at the seed stage. But cash is oxygen for a start-up. More cash gives you more chances to survive. And if I were to do it again, I would have tried to raise $5 million in cash at a $20 million valuation right at the seed stage by demonstrating a bolder vision for the company. With more funding, we would have created more delightful communal experiences for kids from the start, such as gamification, community and group projects, which would make kids even more excited about doing projects and hence, improve their creative learning outcomes.
- Your valuation/ownership chart reflects your daily values: I received constant feedback along my journey that I diluted too much equity to investors as an experienced executive (47 per cent investor ownership at Series A itself!) or had allocated too much ESOP (Employee Stock Ownership Plan) to employees (19 per cent, 1.5 to two times the norm) for a solo founder. But I knew at the onset that I was building for:
    - **Speed**: I closed both my funding rounds within thirty days each, allowing WhiteHat Jr to build superfast and not become a prolonged, long-drawn fundraising, optimizing for ownership and valuations.

      Speed for us was a strategy rather than an execution choice. We were among the last to arrive in a crowded education technology category, where all the major players had already raised tens of millions of dollars of funding. But thanks to speed, by the time competitors realized that coding for kids could be a major category, it was already gone.

- **Team on a Mission**: I wanted all our top talent to be 'owners not renters' in the mission and feel as intensely about the company as I did. So I doubled the ESOP pool (19 per cent) at the seed stage against a typical cap table of 10–15 per cent.

  I would attribute the entire WhiteHat Jr blitz-scaling from 0 to $100 million revenue in eighteen months, where the whole team went over and above daily, to this culture of speed and ownership.

  We never celebrated staying late in office but now after the exit, I hear almost all the old employees talking wistfully about the daily midnight dinner orders from Swiggy for months as we tackled one scaling problem or the other together. Work never felt like work. Everyone came in at 10 a.m. and often left past midnight, deeply energized, experiencing a state of flow from extreme ownership of their work, whether founder, C-level executive or entry-level employee. Your principles may be different but be conscious about them since they'll shape your company's actions daily.

Finally, does Investor Fear of Missing Out (FOMO) drive valuations?

Yes, there's greed and fear in fundraising, as is every part of human nature. In both my funding rounds, getting multiple offers drove up significant interest for WhiteHat Jr, sometimes more so than the fundamentals themselves.

> *'An empty pageant; a stage play; flocks of sheep; a bone flung among a pack of dogs; ants, loaded and labouring; mice, scared and scampering; puppets jerking on their strings; this is life. In the midst of it all, you must take your stand, good-temperedly and without disdain.'*
>
> —Marcus Aurelius, *Meditations*

Figure 11.4: Emperor Marcus Aurelius

Source: 'Emperor Marcus Aurelius', adapted from Shutterstock, by Toby Barton, 29 April 2022. Available at https://www.shutterstock.com

Copyright 2003-2022 by Shutterstock, Inc.

Yet, I walked away with very deep respect for the fundraising and valuation process. I'd run P&Ls many times in my jobs before, but even as head of Discovery India, I'd never looked at a business in as much depth—CAC:LTV, cohort renewals and retention, and fully loaded unit economics—as I learnt to do from our investors. They studied the monthly numbers in as much detail as our team and with their experiences across portfolio companies, always got to the root cause of the one metric that was not going right, sometimes more sharply than us. In one board meeting, our investors rolled up their sleeves for hours to sketch every detail of our product funnel from the time a user first saw a Facebook advertisement to when they renewed classes after the initial purchase and identified how to make each step better rather than merely giving generic advice. As a result, I felt that their valuations accurately reflected the reality of our business and the scope of my ambitions.

All in all, I found everyone, from investors to employees to customers, going over and above to rally behind a vision for a new, better world. And a start-up's value will eventually shrink or expand in proportion to the smallness or bigness of this vision. So always keep it big!

My Mistake

I was too quick to undersell my vision in 2018 after early scepticism from friends and family, negatively impacting our funding and valuation at the seed stage.

With more funding—$5 million versus $1.3 million—I would've built a stronger product and technology team, ensuring an outstanding user experience from the start rather than relying on users being forgiving because of our first-mover advantage.

Your Learnings

Always present a big and obvious vision:

- Magnitude: Does it transcend categories and countries?
- Depth: Does it meet a deep, unexpressed human need?

If not, dig deeper and make it as big as you can make it, and never hesitate to present it as such.

12

Phase 1: 10x Product

Start-up Starter Kit Number 5

How to Start Up with No Co-founder

Do you have a big ownership idea but no co-founder? You should go for it!

Get to the market fast without hunting for the perfect co-founder.

I was told that you needed a co-founder to get venture capital funding when I started. But the reality is more nuanced. Here I share some lessons learnt on how to start up without a co-founder if you don't have one.

First, why do investors typically insist on co-founders?

Start-ups are hard. A venture capitalist from a Russian fund told me once that they never invest in single founders, as a rule, because they've seen solo founders crack and quit quickly from pressure. Psychology aside, functionally, too, every start-up needs three roles in a founding team—a hacker, a designer and a marketer.[1]

HACKER, DESIGNER, MARKETER

The founder is typically the designer, who conceptualizes the complete product, and will perhaps do *either one* of the other two roles well—either the hacker (tech) or the marketer (business) role.

The co-founder does the other role.

How do you find a tech co-founder if you're an MBA (Master of Business Administration) who's spent almost two decades in business as I was?

My traditional networks ran dry quickly, so I reached out 1:1 to anyone who worked in Amazon, Google, Facebook, and other top technology companies from my LinkedIn connections (Figure 12.1). But no luck.

Figure 12.1: LinkedIn outreach to weak connections

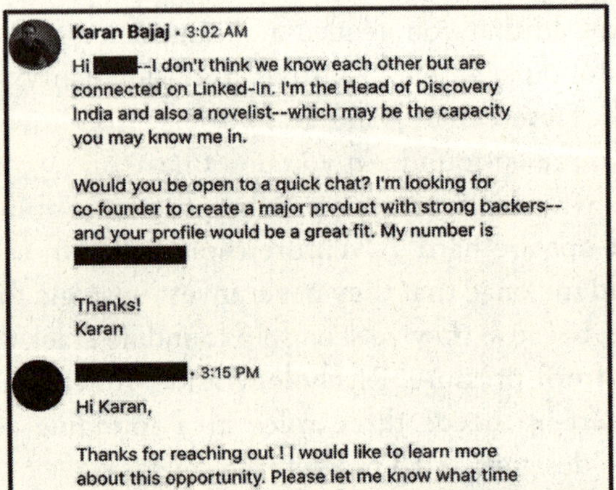
Karan Bajaj • 3:02 AM

Hi ████--I don't think we know each other but are connected on Linked-In. I'm the Head of Discovery India and also a novelist--which may be the capacity you may know me in.

Would you be open to a quick chat? I'm looking for co-founder to create a major product with strong backers--and your profile would be a great fit. My number is ████████

Thanks!
Karan

████████ • 3:15 PM

Hi Karan,

Thanks for reaching out ! I would like to learn more about this opportunity. Please let me know what time

Source: Provided by the author

You can't find an ace co-founder on demand. And beyond competence, you're looking for mad conviction in the idea, co-location, comfort with throwing away everything on an instinct; any one of these is hard to find, leave alone all three.

I spent a month looking for a co-founder while doing my prototype in parallel. I met good people. But I knew good wouldn't be enough. So I decided to go solo.

A good decision, in retrospect, even though I didn't know the Start-up Power Law back then (Figure 12.2).

The Start-up Power Law

Unlike regular jobs where people cluster around the mean with exceptions in either direction (normal distribution), start-ups follow a power law.[1]

Figure 12.2: Power Law: extreme talent concentration

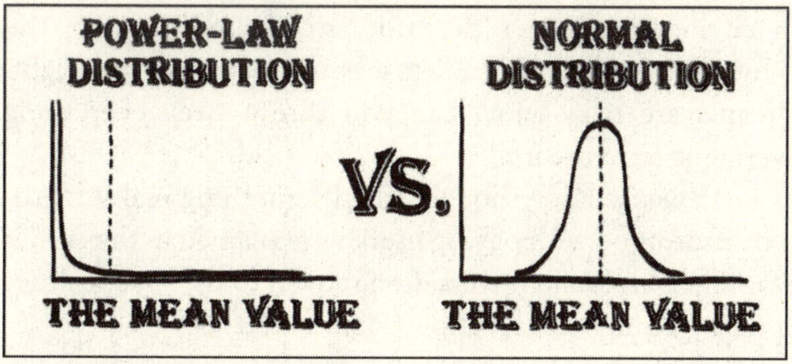

Source: Created by the author

The best people generate an extraordinarily insane amount of value. Ten per cent of hyper-performers generate almost 90 per cent of start-up output.

One great hire can change a start-up's destiny. And WhiteHat Jr's scaling was entirely due to a few of these hires in tech, product and business.

Is your prospective co-founder truly an extreme power-law value generator? If not, go solo. And recruit strong middle management to get your company started while you search long and hard, without desperation, for your co-founder or C-level hires.

How to Recruit the Top 1 Per Cent Middle Management to Get Your Company Started?

Build Traction with Zero-Code/Low-Code Prototype Immediately

I requested my childhood friend in Google to join me as an engineering leader the moment I came up with the WhiteHat Jr idea. He said it was too risky. He was right. Dreams are risky. How can you throw away everything overnight for a dream?

Four weeks later, though, I had something real. A zero-code prototype with paying users, as explained in the earlier chapters. Now, our conversation moved to the practicalities of salary, equity and location (Figure 12.3).

Figure 12.3: WhiteHat Jr's first prototype

Source: Provided by the author

Turn your dream into reality now.

Life punishes the vague wish and rewards the specific ask[3], and so does talent! Don't tell a prospective engineering head that you have an idea. Show them your prototype to close the deal. You'll win even if they don't sign up. My friend still didn't join but our early traction helped the company get going. Or else it would still be a dream.

Attract Top Talent with Hackers and Painters/ 30x7 Rule

Paul Graham, head of Y Combinator, considers top tech talent akin to artists. And I too found our top engineering hires surprisingly similar to the writers I knew from my fiction days. Beyond moodiness(!), the best tech folks, like artists, are motivated most by:

- Creation: Am I creating true, new-to-the-world IP or solving the toughest technical problems?
- Scale: Will my creation be used by a very large number of users and impact them positively?

Convince top technology talent on IP by ensuring that your technical vision is as big and obvious as your business vision. For example, a technical goal I articulated in the early days was enabling parents to understand their kids better by applying machine-learning algorithms on thousands of hours of live classes daily. At WhiteHat Jr, kids did analytical, mathematical, creative and artistic activities in each coding class. With visual recognition software, we could identify what kind of activities made a kid spike in joy, as seen by their hand movements becoming more energetic or their facial expressions changing. We would therefore be able to guide parents on whether their kids were more analytically or creatively inclined, mathematical or abstract thinkers, and how to foster that by suggesting a range of projects that nurtured that skill. All engineers were excited by the impactful problem statement and how technically complex yet creative the challenge was.

For convincing talent on scale, show extreme conviction in your growth. We got all our first twenty hires from LinkedIn jobs, where I wrote the job descriptions (JDs) myself and reached out to applicants via WhatsApp individually. We were seven people in the living room of my house, and yet our JDs reflected complete conviction in our future even then (Figure 12.4).

Figure 12.4: Early WhiteHat Jr LinkedIn JDs

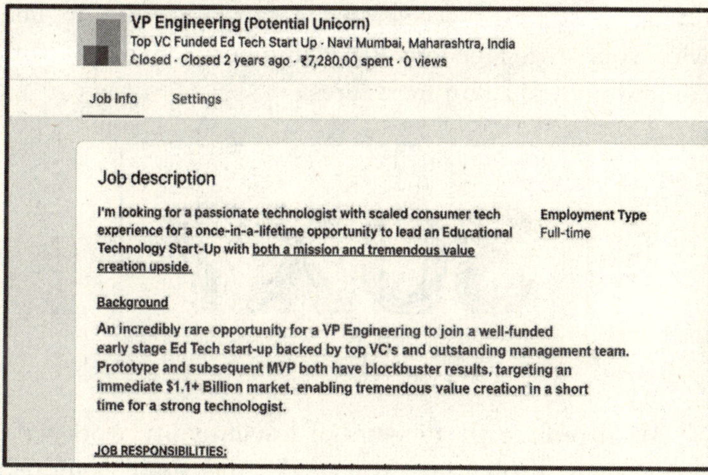

VP Engineering (Potential Unicorn)
Top VC Funded Ed Tech Start Up · Navi Mumbai, Maharashtra, India
Closed · Closed 2 years ago · ₹7,280.00 spent · 0 views

Job Info Settings

Job description

I'm looking for a passionate technologist with scaled consumer tech experience for a once-in-a-lifetime opportunity to lead an Educational Technology Start-Up with both a mission and tremendous value creation upside.

Employment Type
Full-time

Background

An incredibly rare opportunity for a VP Engineering to join a well-funded early stage Ed Tech start-up backed by top VC's and outstanding management team. Prototype and subsequent MVP both have blockbuster results, targeting an immediate $1.1+ Billion market, enabling tremendous value creation in a short time for a strong technologist.

JOB RESPONSIBILITIES:

Source: Provided by the author

Top hackers follow the same extreme power law as artists. The best coders are 100 times more productive than the average ones. So, hiring top tech talent is probably your single-most important call at the start of the company.

HACKERS AND PAINTERS

Source: Paul Graham[4]

Top business talent motivations are simpler as they are driven most by an accelerated career trajectory. In line with your own Freedom Rule Number 3, make a 30x7 commitment to all business hires:

30X7

'We'll replace thirty years of low-intensity work with seven years of high-intensity work. And you'll compress thirty years of personal and professional growth in these seven years.'

Follow the '3,3,3' Recruiting Rule to Find Top Talent Yourself

A founder's single-biggest leverage in the company is to find a great team, so I spent an inordinate amount of time recruiting myself, following this 3x3x3 rule:

THREE RECRUITERS

I was in direct touch with three recruiters, exchanging hundreds of WhatsApp messages with them, through the three years of running the company. None of them were the usual marquee names such as Korn Ferry and Michael Page, but they understood our values, our speed, and our energy deeply, and grew with us (Figure 12.5).

Figure 12.5: Founders-in-scaling: 24x7 recruiter contact

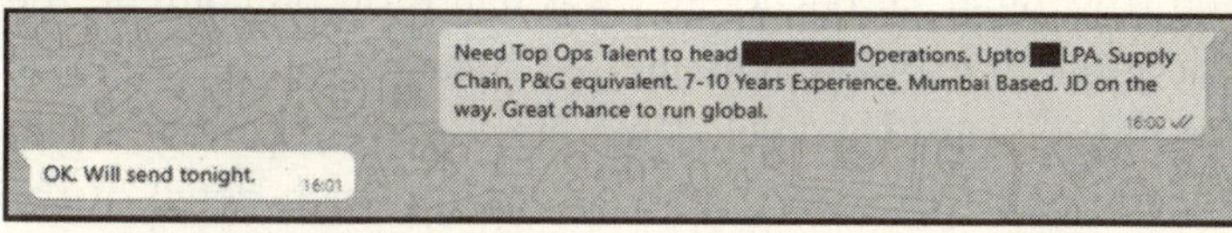

Source: Provided by the author

I highly recommend having a few key, deep recruiting relationships, helmed by an ace in-house management recruiter, to get first access to top talent. You can reach out to these recruiters who helped me recruit more than forty middle and senior management leaders, including the chief operating officer (COO) and chief technology officer (CTO), in record time who show the same 24×7 zeal as the founders:

1. Tarun Bhagarva: tarun.bhagarva@talentgen.co.in
2. Gorakh Tiwari: Gorakh@vedaconsulting.co.in
3. Prashant Sardana: prashant.sardana@steergrowth.in

THREE INTERVIEW QUESTIONS

These three questions, among others, helped me gauge for start-up fit:

A. What are your improvement areas?

Rationale: Start-ups are brutal, and folks with low self-awareness struggle to learn fast. Reject anyone who gives superficial answers such as 'I'm not good at promoting myself' and 'I have to learn how to network better'. The best talent is brutally self-aware. For instance, when I was asked by the managing director of Nexus in the IC meeting what I would do differently as WhiteHat Jr CEO than I did as Discovery's head, I was open about my shortcomings. I'd been too naive and trusting at Discovery and was hands-off on content, the fulcrum of a television channel. As a leader, you can delegate but not abdicate. I had failed in projects where I had abdicated my responsibility. Now, I would get into each detail of the product and build it with my own hands at WhiteHat Jr.

B. Where can our business model go wrong?

Rationale: Your best hires will be the ones who believe in the mission but challenge the founder's irrational conviction often! The answer to this question shows both preparation depth and independent thinking. I hired our first curriculum head, for example, because he kept asking me penetrating questions on the business model and margin structure as well as the competitive moat of our content daily for one week after I interviewed him until he was fully convinced that I knew what I was doing.

C. What are you reading/learning now?

Rationale: The best folks are always learning and striving to get better. Anyone who draws a blank at this question will perhaps not have the continuous curiosity needed for a start-up.

THREE REFERENCES

I would call candidate references myself to get a three-dimensional sense of the hire. References are golden. I would always ask references whether they would rate the employee among the top 1 per cent, 5 per cent, 10 per cent, 25 per cent, or 50 per cent of people they have ever worked with. I knew less than top 5 per cent wouldn't work for the pace I was setting. Once, for example, I was about to give an offer to a candidate with a stellar résumé—IIT, Wharton, Amazon, top ed tech start-up—for a pivotal role of a teacher operations head role. The résumé was such a good fit, and interviews with both our investors and me were so positive, that I almost didn't do the references. At the last minute, however, I decided to stick to my 3x3x3 principle and called his references. All three of the references rated him between the top 10 per cent and top 25 per cent of people they'd worked with. He was good at executing set processes but struggled to set up new systems from scratch. I dropped him and restarted the hiring process despite the urgency for the role with our rapidly growing teacher base. A start-up leadership role is unlike any you've done before. You're creating *and* running the wheel daily rather than just running the wheel, as you do in an established organization. I knew he wouldn't succeed with us. Later, my instinct turned out to be correct. The hire bounced from one hot start-up to another, unable to make sense of the inevitable chaos in a start-up.

3,3,3

Now for the Money Question, Can You Raise Venture Funding Without a Co-founder?

Yes!

As I shared in the previous section, venture capitalists fund any start-up that delivers:

1. A 'Big and Obvious' vision for *tomorrow*.
2. A strong business *today*.

Your founding team becomes a proxy in the absence of a number two, that is, a business, at the seed stage. Can you overcome their co-founder hesitation by showing early traction and a passionate mid-management team (Figure 12.6)?

Figure 12.6: WhiteHat Jr seed 'traction' slide

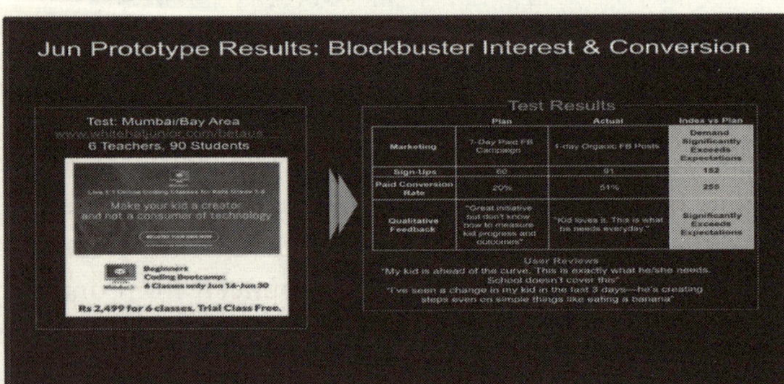

Source: Provided by the author

Remember, you'll always be out of time in hiring key management roles in a start-up. But always commit to hiring A-category players. Until then, keep the role open. One wrong hire can set you back by months, which is life or death for a start-up.

> *'But if you don't find an intelligent companion, a wise and well-meaning person, going the same way as yourself, then walk alone. Like a king abandoning a conquered kingdom or like a great elephant in the deep forest. It is better to be alone than to be with those who will hinder your progress.'*
>
> —The Buddha

Figure 12.7: The wise Buddha

Source: 'Buddha Meditation', adapted from Shutterstock, by Chandni Chauhan, 26 April 2022, available at https://www.shutterstock.com Copyright 2003–2022 by Shutterstock, Inc.

During the time the role is open, approach every function you don't know with first principles. For example, one of my profound early experiences at WhiteHat Jr was sitting with our first back-end developer and understanding how he was setting up our database architecture by asking specific, detailed questions without worrying about looking silly as a CEO. As he answered my questions patiently, a light dawned on me. Complex-sounding technical words like 'database architecture' were mostly a reflection of our business vision and strategy. You can organize a database in line with how users navigate your product, starting with their names and phone numbers to their kids' grade, course type and curriculum version. As the founder, I was therefore best positioned to help create our database architecture even if I knew nothing about the technical act of creating it.

My fear of tech turned to understanding and my reticence about things I didn't know to active participation in every function from that day. And knowing that I could understand new fields and keep things moving forward fast by asking detailed, seemingly silly questions without fear, and figuring out solutions together with junior functional owners, allowed me to wait for an excellent CTO rather than rush to pick an average co-founder.

My Mistakes

The founder's strength becomes the weakness of the organization. A founder typically hires last for the functions they're experienced in, thinking they can run the function easily. This is a big mistake. The founder has to hold the whole company together, creating both a vision for the future and being involved in the deepest details today, and has no time to run an individual function.

With a decade of brand building in Procter & Gamble and Kraft, I thought I would set up our marketing function easily when it was time. It was never time! WhiteHat Jr's brand-building was handled by interns and junior marketers, with me coming in and out of marketing, right until BYJU's acquisition. As a result, several of our social media campaigns were off-tone and our internal marketing review systems were too weak to catch our mistakes. We lacked the gravitas of the committed education company we were and paid the price for it with severe public criticism for WhiteHat Jr's marketing. It was entirely my mistake. For a $100 million company, I should've hired a brand-building leader early instead of hiring strong leaders only to offset my lack of experience in product, technology and curriculum.

Your Learnings

Hire for your own strengths early and not just for your knowledge gaps. As a rule of thumb, beyond the early stages of the company, if you're sitting in any functional meeting where the follow-up items from the meeting are coming to you, you're late in hiring the functional leader. The founder should lead every function, but none directly.

13

Start-up Starter Kit Number 6

How to Find Product–Market Fit Fast in a Start-up

IN February 2019, four months into officially starting WhiteHat Jr, I picked up a customer service call in the middle of a meeting with Omidyar Networks, one of our seed investors. I fixed the customer's live-class camera issue, guiding them step by step to download Google Chrome's latest update and allowing camera permission for the WhiteHat Jr Chrome extension. The investor looked at me with incredulity and asked me the same question everyone was asking me during this time: Why wasn't I building a team despite having seed funding? Later, they asked it more impatiently: Why was I so slow in hiring even for entry-level positions? Had I really headed a business before at Discovery?

You need to hit product–market fit to scale. We weren't ready yet.

Your users need to *love* your product, not just like it. Without your users' positive word-of-mouth publicity, your start-up will enter a self-destructive spiral of rising customer acquisition costs, leading to more funds being diverted to marketing and less to product, which in turn makes word-of-mouth publicity even more elusive.

Keep costs unforgivingly low until you hit product–market fit, even if it means the CEO answering customer service calls for months.

How to hit product–market fit fast in a start-up so that your company can scale and achieve its destiny? Follow this three-step approach:

Define Your Product–Market Fit Metric Mathematically

We launched WhiteHat Jr's Beta version in December 2018, one month into incorporating the company. One thousand users signed up for a trial and we had 150 paying customers by 1 January 2019. We did our first NPS[1] survey among the 150 users one week after classes began. The results were disappointing.

Among the three courses we launched, one for Grade 1, one for Grades 2 and 3, one for Grades 4, 5 and 6, we had scores of –12, 0 and 50, respectively. An NPS of 50 is gold standard, and anything less than 25 is a disaster. Only one course was working. We doubled down with urgency. Without a 10x product, I knew no revenue would come in to offset expenses, so we would just keep burning cash monthly.

Our seven-member team visited the homes of fifty of our first 150 customers to understand exactly how they were using the product. One mother showed me how her seven-year-old daughter cleaned up her study desk thirty minutes before class because she was so excited to meet her teacher as she had never experienced a 1:1 class online before. Parents had rarely seen their kids so engaged in any activity, but we had many improvements to make.

Our live classes varied in length based on the student–teacher interaction, but parents wanted them to last a minimum of forty-five minutes so that they could schedule their own days better. We immediately added additional activities that teachers could include in class if students were finishing the class before the allotted one hour time. Kids wanted projects after class to practise their skills beyond the projects they were already doing in class. We added multiple projects at the end of each class. Both parents and kids wanted more time with the teacher after class to resolve doubts, so we made doubt-resolution classes a part of the curriculum. We built new features furiously, calling children to our office each evening when they returned from school to test them out.

The next NPS crossed 25 for each course. We were still far from the goal and visited more users' homes and made more improvements. During this time, we cut all unnecessary costs to keep our cash burn low. We didn't even switch on the AC on the weekends—a seven-member team doesn't need AC!

Five months after the start of the company in March 2019, in the sixth version of the product, we hit a target NPS of 50 in each course. Then, we knew the product was ready and scaled from a team of seven to one of 3,000-plus and from a revenue of less than $1 million to more than $100 million over the next eighteen months.

A start-up needs extreme patience in the beginning to create a 10x product, then extreme impatience to scale it 10x. Know the exact metrics that will trigger your crossover from patience to impatience. I'd defined these metrics from the first day of the company:

- **50 per cent NPS:** World-class product standard.
- **50 per cent revenue from referrals:** Users love us enough to refer their friends and family to us, reducing our customer acquisition cost by half.
- **50 per cent renewal rates:** Users wanted to keep using more of the product.

50-50-50

Define Your Alternative World

Strong NPS, referrals and revenues were all indicators of a great product—and we wanted all three. Your product–market metrics may be different based on your business model but define them at the start to relentlessly keep building and iterating until you hit them. Or you'll be distracted by investor pressure or your own internal panic to scale prematurely, one of the leading causes of start-up failure.[2]

Be 10x Superior to Your Users' Alternative World

In one of our first WhiteHat Jr rejections, a top venture capitalist firm principal told me that he had done a thorough Google keyword search and no one was searching 'coding for kids'. The idea was too small.

It was the wrong search term. Parents engaged their kids after school in neighbourhood playdates, ballet classes, art projects, Vedic mathematics and chess lessons in early childhood. They didn't know yet that they wanted coding for kids. But they wanted their kids to be deeply absorbed in a creative, joyful activity that had cognitive benefits, and they felt that none of these activities were fully delivering those for kids. Our job was to simply create a 10x alternative to the disorganized creative development market in India. Hence, we quickly understood the user's burning pains from the alternative world by calling or physically meeting the people who signed up for our very first trial classes:

- Kids almost uniformly lost interest in activities such as ballet, Lego and art over time because they kept repeating the same activities in each class.
- Parents found teacher quality and engagement inconsistent, even in heavy skill-based subjects like Vedic mathematics and chess. Parents would often pay for a three-month-long course with weekly classes in advance, and the kid would not like the teacher in the first class and stop attending.
- Parents and kids both disliked commuting after school for hobby classes, given the increasing traffic in big cities.

Our product would be 10x if we solved just these problems. As a result, we focused on building and improving just three features daily:

- A creative curriculum where kids could both learn new concepts and create a tangible output at the end of each class to feel a sense of accomplishment in what they learnt. In each class or over multiple classes, they would build a game, an app and later, full-fledged digital products.
- A standardized operations process to select highly qualified and empathetic teachers, the top 1 per cent among the applicants.
- A robust technical scheduling engine that allowed parents to schedule and reschedule live classes with one click as per a kid's convenience.

10X

That's all we needed, and a seven-member team with three hackers, three curriculum designers and me, was enough to build it. We didn't need to add more teams and costs. Once I met a new investor during this period, who told me how an education technology platform they had invested in was building a breakthrough new video solution and another was aggregating all well-known IIT teachers in a large marketplace. Did we have a road map for such breakthrough features?

No! Parents weren't asking for better Zoom software for video or an IIT teacher at an exorbitant cost. They wanted their kid to create and learn. The investor thought I wasn't visionary enough. But your only vision should be to delight your user ten times more than their current state.

What is your product's alternative world? Define it clearly and build a maximum of three features that deliver a 10x experience versus the alternative. You'll create both a new category and a new meaning in the world. And survive on Maggi noodles until then, working with a lean team and cutting all costs relentlessly (maybe not ACs!) so that you can use all your funding for scaling as below.

Hit Meaningful Scale with Marketing Iteration

All the investors who had rejected us at the seed stage gave us term sheets within two weeks when we went to raise our Series A around six months later in June 2019. They weren't just attracted by a superior product, but now we also had scale. Immediately after we hit our 50/50/50 product metrics in March 2019, we increased our marketing spends significantly for three months to add thousands of paying customers and show that our strong product metrics held at scale. We demonstrated that we had what it took to build a new category from scratch in this world.

Our product–market fit was therefore established over two steps:

Phase 1: Product Iteration

Success Metric: 50 per cent NPS/ 50 per cent referral revenue/ 50 per cent renewals.
Timing: November 2018–March 2019.
Number of Paying Users: 1,000 over five months.

Phase 2: Marketing Iteration

Success Metric: Rs 1 crore monthly revenue; continued 50/50/50 metrics.
Timing: April–June 2019.
Number of Paying Users: 5,000 over three months.

Without scale from Phase 2, we would have gone back and forth on the same questions on market size that we were asked at the seed stage.

Inevitably, however, our monthly cash burn increased from Rs 10 lakh in Phase 1 to more than Rs 1 crore in Phase 2. With an influx of users, we had to invest in call-centre teams to solve live class issues, post-sales support to answer user queries on classes and learning outcomes, and mid-level management to manage these teams. In the beginning, these processes were manual and costly since we followed a cycle, as most start-ups do, of understanding problems by putting people on it, then creating efficient processes to solve them, and finally automating solutions with product and technology.

How do you define meaningful scale for your start-up? Is it thousands of users or Rs 1 crore/month revenue or any other metric in line with your model?

Select your scale metric conclusively to prove that you will take your new-to-the-world category from the edges to the centre. But start scaling with marketing only after you've hit your product metrics, or else you'll run out of cash. Start-ups are like riding a tiger. Ride it too fast and you'll stumble, fall and get swallowed. Too slow, though, and you'll be swallowed as well. I hope this helps you get it just right.

My Mistake

We were very disciplined in Phase 1 (product iteration) but lost focus on marketing messaging during Phase 2 (marketing iteration).

'Indian masses won't pay for online coding classes. It's not core.' I'd heard this message so many times that I wasn't fully confident about communicating our core message of kids being builders and creators for life in every creative endeavour. Instead, we threw the kitchen sink at marketing, doing Facebook advertisements and YouTube videos on career-oriented messages like how artificial intelligence was the future of work, and urgency messages on limited spots for free trial.

These typical functional messages missed out on one fundamental human reality: *We're all living our stories.* We're all looking to survive, thrive, grow, and find the deepest meaning of why we're here. It doesn't matter if you're rich or poor, metro or non-metro, an urban user or not; you're looking for meaning and truth. Six months into our Series A in March 2020, when we did a thorough quantitative analysis of our Facebook advertising performance, we saw our best performing advertising was also closest to the mission of the company. Advertisements that talked unapologetically about kids becoming *creators for life* with coding and the *touch of beauty* creation brought to a child's soul performed the best.

They did well in the US test market and India. The Indian masses cared as much about creation and beauty as the Americans.

We returned to our creation message, but the brand had been heavily diluted by the inconsistent and often off-tone messaging.

Your Learning

Communicate only the highest human need your 10x product offers. How does your product help meet your users' deepest human yearning of surviving, thriving, growing and finding meaning? You'll have an obvious answer if you have a 10x product. Just articulate that to users uninhibitedly, without reservation. Users will always embrace your product's highest truth because you add truth and meaning to their lives.

14

Phases 2 and 3: Systems Set-up and Scaling

Start-up Starter Kit Number 7

How to Scale a Company

Three Tools That Work

THREE months into our Series A in January 2020, a large ed tech player poached our teachers and knocked off our exact curriculum, down to the curriculum PDF formatting. I complained to our common investors. It wasn't fair. We had created the coding category, after all. Our competitor had been in the industry for almost a decade and had raised hundreds of millions of dollars in funding. Why did they have to rip off a small Series A start-up? Shouldn't our common board member intervene?

I was wrong to complain. No one cares. It's an open market. Everyone was noticing our momentum. If we were slow to scale, others would do it faster.

Start-ups at early stages live in days, not decades.

Scale one month too early and you'll lose all your money since your product is not ready. One month too late, however, and players with ten times your funding enter and make you redundant in the category *you created*. You have to blitz-scale the moment you know you've created a category. Anything less is a lack of conviction.

We had hit product–market fit, achieving our 50/50/50 goal at scale, and then built robust systems to scale over the next few months. So now, we doubled every month, going from $10 million annual revenue run rate in February 2020 to $100 million annual revenue run rate in August 2020.

The large education player tried to scale using our curriculum during this period. But in a two-way platform, teachers congregate where students are and students, in turn, go where the best teachers are. Kids were already telling other kids in their school about WhiteHat Jr, and this phenomenon multiplied as we scaled. As a result, the teachers poached by our competitor had few students to teach on their platform. They came back to us. We had set such a scorching pace that the competitor couldn't keep up despite their higher funding and aggressive tactics, and stepped out after a bit, as did other large players who entered the segment.

How do you scale systems fast enough to meet user growth? I found almost no playbook to learn from during WhiteHat Jr's condensed hyper-scaling phase, so here I share three tools that worked for start-ups and businesses on fast trajectories:

Your Management Dashboard: What Gets Measured Gets Managed

We hit our first $1 million revenue month at midnight on 31 March 2020. Fifty out of 200 employees were still in office. The office erupted in celebration. We'd always spoken of the $1 million milestone as the dividing line between being a niche category creator and a mainstream education player. Our analyses showed that other education players had reached this milestone a minimum of five years after inception and spending $50–100 million. We'd reached there in fifteen months while spending less than $2 million. We were going mainstream. Our dream of making every kid a creator with coding was now poised to be a reality. Everyone was ecstatic. Except the management team.

We'd just got wind from an advance look at the next day's management dashboard that a code break in our communication system had led to emails not being triggered to customers for four hours. In our growth phase, 70 per cent of our revenue came from new users and 30 per cent from renewals. Without email prompts, trial user attendance would dip by a third in subsequent days and revenue would go down proportionately. Our CTO got working on the bug immediately, fixing it by 4 a.m. so that we wouldn't lose more than a day of revenue.

How do you track every relevant detail of your company in real time? Measure every metric that matters. And review it daily without fail (Figure 14.1).

Figure 14.1: WhiteHat Jr management dashboard: Sample (reviewed daily for three years and counting)

DASHBOARD	Date(D-1) (MM-DD-YYYY)	Last Week Same Day (MM-DD-YYYY)	%change	WTD (MM-DD-YYYY)	LWTD (MM-DD-YYYY)	%change	MTD (MM-DD-YYYY)	LMTD (MM-DD-YYYY)	%change
				From Date	From Date		From Date	From Date	
	-Sep	-Sep		13-Sep	-Sep		-Sep	-Aug	
				15-Sep			-Sep	-Aug	
			-3%			2%			-32%
			4%			10%			266%
			6%			14%			5%
			-4%			1%			-9%
			60%			106%			50%
			76%			3%			63%
			76%			-4%			59%
			-			-			-
			0%			3%			-15%
			-7%			-5%			-18%
			16%			17%			67%
			3%			2%			-11%
			6%			5%			-19%
			-			0%			0%

Source: Provided by the author

Your management dashboard should have two types of metrics: Level one output metrics, such as revenue and customer satisfaction scores, updated daily; and detailed Level 2 input metrics such as email open rates and call-centre attendance. Monitoring Level 2 enables you to diagnose Level 1 problems immediately.

Follow this metric 'Rule of Three' to always be on top of issues, mostly before they arise:

1. Measure every metric that matters daily.
2. Have an owner for each metric.
3. Review every metric daily in a management meeting.

We met daily from 10 to 11 a.m., without fail, to review the management dashboard, from the start of the company. All twenty members of the management team attended, from the curriculum head to product vertical owners to the teacher recruitment and operations lead to the CTO and senior sales executives, which kept everyone marching together to solve the blitz of blitz-scaling problems in real time.

Your Organization Structure: Are You Creating Legends?

Our first vice president of sales had started in our call centre as an entry-level employee. He moved from call-centre executive to call-centre leader, then to sales executive, sales team leader, sales director and sales vice president within eighteen months.

Break traditional management rules in a start-up. In line with Rule 3, you make a 30/7 commitment to people who've signed up for your mission in a start-up.

'We'll replace thirty years of low-intensity work with seven years of high-intensity work. And you'll compress thirty years of personal and professional growth in these seven years.'

30X7

Promote people fast to scale the organization fast. The moment we decided to scale 10x in January 2020, we asked our six young sales team leaders who were leading teams of twelve each then to elevate themselves to vice presidents, who would lead teams of 150–180 each within eight weeks. We just laid out a symmetrical organization blueprint structure from them:

- Each vice president would have three directors reporting to them.
- Each director would have six team leaders.
- Each team leader would have ten sales managers reporting to them.

Within this blueprint, the vice president would act as a mini-CEO, working directly with recruiters and human resources to recruit, offer and train new hires. The team leaders were all in their twenties with no pedigrees, but in almost every case, they delivered because of their overwhelming passion for the company, our mission and their own extraordinary growth.

Organization structure is the single-best tool to scale start-ups. Do you really need to wait for six months for a pedigreed, experienced hire from outside the company for a leadership role?

In some cases, when you're setting a complex new operation or system from scratch, the answer is yes. In most cases, however, when you're executing fast and strong against a blueprint, don't go with the default IIT/IIM external hires. Make legends within the organization. And they'll inspire the next generation of driven, hungry young people to become legends.

Your Systems: Are They as Simple as You Can Make Them?

Past midnight, one day in September 2019, my CTO, operations head, product lead and I were debating the relative pros and cons of Salesforce vs LeadSquared to manage our sales for the tenth time. I wish I knew then what I know now: *It doesn't matter.*

Make system decisions in days rather than months. I learnt it the hard way. We had hit product–market fit in June 2019, but part of what held us back from scaling immediately was our indecisiveness on selecting the right systems for the company. Just like sales, we had similar debates on call centre outsourcing and post-sales telephony. Eventually, we took a decision when we made a firm commitment to scale in November 2019, and immediately after setting up our systems, we understood that any large well-reviewed SaaS (Software as a Service) provider can meet 80 per cent of your use cases. And your in-house engineering team has to develop the remaining 20 per cent.

Speed is your lifeblood. Simplify to scale. And seldom build in-house systems that SaaS companies have spent years perfecting.

> *'Simplify! One does not accumulate but eliminate.*
> *It is not daily increase but daily decrease'*
>
> —Bruce Lee

Figure 14.1: Bruce Lee in contemplation

'Bruce Lee, Martial Artist", adapted from "Pixabay", by stevenbatty, 7 November, 2021, from https://pixabay.com.

Over the next year, we went on to manage more than 5 million users and over 40,000 daily live classes across students from more than 100 countries with just a few key systems listed below. And rarely, if ever, did we face issues we couldn't solve.

- Telephony: Ameyo/Exotel (India), TalkDesk (outside India)
- Sales: Salesforce
- Post-sales support: ZenDesk

My Mistake: Not Understanding the Founder's Role Evolution

A founder's role evolves rapidly in a start-up in the following phases:

- 0–1 Building phase: The founder is the first product manager and owns each small detail of the product-pre-product–market fit.
- 1–100 Scaling phase: The founder as the business systems expert should become a student of systems to blitz-scale recruiting, sales, operations, tech, all functions.
- 100–1,000 Steady-state phase: The founder as the culture champion should hire leaders stronger than themselves to lead every function and focus their energy on scaling organization culture.

I did 0–1 and 1–100 well but was late to enter the 100–1,000 leadership phase since I continued being heavily engaged in daily operations, more out of my interest than for adding meaningful value. As a result, the company's cultural fabric weakened during the scaling phase. Our attrition rates, historically low, hit industry levels. For the first time, we had sales managers mis-sell users on the career benefits of coding instead of talking about the mission of children being creators, not consumers. New mid-level management hires weren't inspiring new recruits with the energy of the original founding team. We were drifting into becoming a mediocre 'just another job' workplace, a far cry from the lofty ideal of creating a world-class company we had at the start.

I corrected this in November 2020, nine months into our scaling, much later than I should have. Over three months, I articulated and disseminated company values within each functional group. I got a culture team in place. The company resurrected again, but I should've never let it reach this point.

Your Learning

For successful scaling, follow these steps:

Define Company Values on Day 1

For too long, I'd considered defining company values to be a theoretical exercise because most values I'd read from other companies were so generic as to be white noise. I should have dug deeper. Defined right, company values can lift and inspire each moment, decision and meeting in a company. The following three principles helped me define meaningful values, and I wished I'd known them on Day 1:

Strengths over Ideals

Your starting point to write iconic values should be to dig deep within yourself and ask yourself what makes you tick as a person as against a theoretical ideal of what you want the company to become. How did you become among the rarest of the rare 10 per cent in the world who became entrepreneurs? What are your strengths, passions and dreams that have brought you this far? For example, Google's 'You can be serious without a suit' value captures their unique collegial ethos.

In digging deep, I realized that my life was characterized by always taking big leaps for increasing my impact on the world, whether it was the decision to write a novel that impacted millions or to take a bid at direct spiritual experience. The company too was built with this ethos; from wanting every kid to be a creator in the world with coding to dreaming of music touching the soul of every kid; '10x Thinking, 10x Impact' became one of our values.

Specific over Generic

In my corporate career, I would often see values like accountability or transparency on posters on walls, but they were too generic to mean anything. So I set out to choose values that truly impacted daily behaviour.

I was inspired by Amazon, which used specific phrases like 'Accomplish more with less' and 'Constraints breed innovation', which made frugality a passion within Amazon. We chose 'Daily improvement' as one of our values, as a result. The value was actionable and direct and reflected our specific actions like the whole management meeting daily at 10 a.m. without fail to make some improvement in our system for the day, whether product enhancements for class experience or adding a new operational process for better sales revenue realization.

Energy over Inspiration

Uber's original values, such as 'Superpumped' and 'Always be hustlin' made your pulse race. They pushed it to a fault perhaps, and yet I admired the act of selecting values that immediately inspired a sense of energy. 'Meritocratic utopia' became one of our values with this principle. I'd rarely faced politics in my corporate career and had aspired to create a company that was completely fair, especially since 75 per cent of our workforce were women. I wanted everyone to feel they could progress in the company without barriers of gender, race and colour.

Based on the above principles, here are WhiteHat Jr's final values:

- Being an owner not a renter
- 10x thinking, 10x impact
- Meritocratic utopia
- Daily improvement
- Impenetrable integrity
- Creating joyful learning experiences

Within weeks of rolling out the values, we could sense an energetic shift. People complimented or corrected each other in meetings when they felt someone was displaying or not displaying a certain value. Leaders highlighted people exhibiting the values in town halls. Our recruitment team had a common language to offer or reject new hires. The organization now had values as a glue to bind us together.

Disseminate Company Values with the 'Rule of Seven'

A message must be communicated seven times before someone hears it once, according to an old maxim. After articulating the values, we built it into seven touchpoints with employees across the whole value chain from entry to exit:

1. Recruitment: Recruiters were trained in evaluating and giving feedback to candidates based on values.
2. Orientation: Values were central in our new hire orientation.
3. Team discussions: Each small team in the organization discussed how they would bring the values to life in their own groups.
4. One-to-one managerial feedback: We encouraged values to become a critical part of the manager–employee one-to-one feedback.
5. Weekly department recognition: Each week, people who had over-performed were highlighted in the department town halls.
6. Quarterly company-wide town halls: We celebrated quarterly value champions in organization-wide town halls.
7. Annual performance appraisal: Values were given 30 per cent weight in performance raises and career progression.

We had a dedicated values and culture leader organizing the above. I recommend hiring one at 300 people instead of waiting as I did until we had more than 3,000 employees.

External Leadership Training

We promoted folks in their early twenties to run large organizations within the company as mini CEOs based on performance alone, supported by very basic in-house managerial training programmes. In retrospect, I would still create legends by promoting exceptional middle managers fast. But I'd complement out-of-turn promotions with rigorous formal leadership training to have consistently strong people leaders in the company. I recommend Shubika Bilkha, a leadership coach, who is transparent and accessible, and helped us work with people's natural strengths to mould them into strong leaders (shubika.bilkha@edpoweru.com).

I hope this helps you get more things right than wrong in your scaling. You'll make your own mistakes in this often-chaotic, always-energizing phase, but you'll look back at this time fondly because of the hundreds of customer lives you touch and the jobs you create along the way.

Epilogue

Your Personal Freedom Manifesto

I awoke with a sense of dread on the day I planned to inform my manager in London about my decision to leave Discovery India in order to establish a start-up. Our meeting got postponed that day because he had a last-minute call with Discovery's global CEO. I was relieved. Perhaps this was a sign from the universe for me to let go of my mid-life crises and find satisfaction in a job 99.9 per cent of people in the world would perhaps give their arms and legs for. I ruminated on the 90 per cent start-up failure risk once again. Who could be so irresponsible at the age of thirty-nine? I didn't even have a start-up idea yet. This was my moment to pull back. Later that week, I met my manager and put in my papers.

The hero has to answer their call to adventure. You find your dharma, your destiny, only when you cross over from the known to the unknown world.

I'd faced this exact hesitation and discomfort when I received the call before to backpack around the world, learn yoga and meditation full-time, and become a novelist. Joseph Campbell's *The Hero's Journey* (1990) helped me understand I wasn't alone.

The Hero's Journey

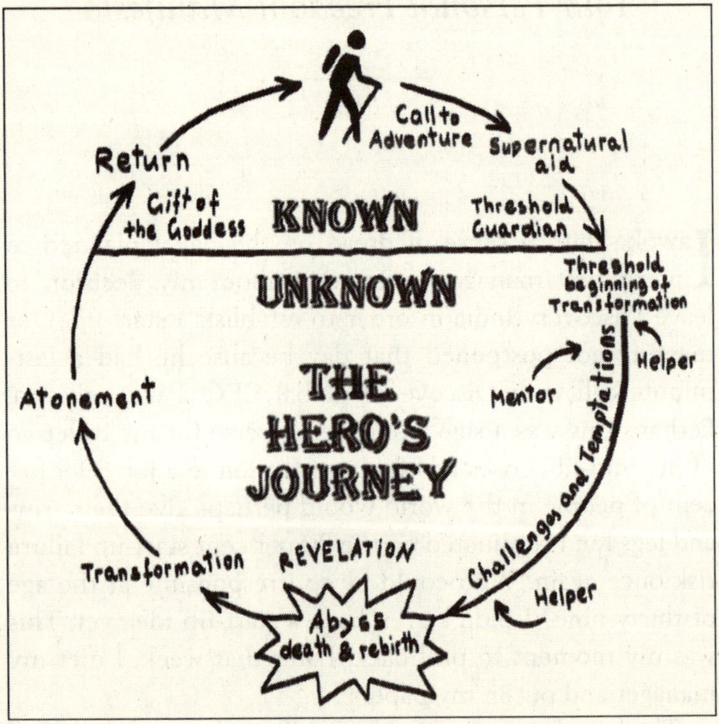

Source: Joseph Campbell

In the beginning, every hero refuses the call to adventure. Then, they cross the threshold into the unknown world.

They're beset by challenges in the unknown world. One day, they'll hit the abyss where all seems lost. Yet, they find the inner reserves to dig deep within themselves and climb out of the darkness. A profound, spiritual transformation occurs from overcoming their hardest struggles. Now, they'll return with the gift of hard-won wisdom that lifts up the world around them.

The Buddha spent years in indecision about leaving his kingdom and family. One night, he crossed the threshold into the life of a seeker. For six years, he wandered homeless, learning, mastering and abandoning the prevailing spiritual rituals. One day, he pushed himself to the brink of death by practising severe austerities, before digging deep within himself to find enlightenment. He returned with the gift of Buddhism, practised by millions around the world more than 2,000 years after his death. Mahatma Gandhi followed this exact hero's journey when he left his comfortable life as an attorney in South Africa to become the sage-fighter that liberated millions from their bondage. My goals were infinitely smaller and my journeys far less heroic, but each of my quests followed the same stages.

The challenges in starting up became clear to me on my very first day of WhiteHat Jr's official launch when none of the first sixty users I called after the free trial wanted to purchase the course. Were the prototype results I got before an aberration, because they were users who'd signed up from our personal Facebook pages and were from the same economic strata as we were? I had a sinking feeling in my stomach. How low had I fallen from being Discovery India's head who had met the country's prime minister for work, to having almost every user I spoke to cut their phone on me at WhiteHat Jr? Would I ever be able to resurrect myself? I pushed forward with great self-doubt.

In my writing life, I hit the abyss in 2014 when I received my sixtieth rejection for *The Seeker*. I was at my wife's parents' home in Florida with my wife's sisters and brothers-in-law and their kids. Everyone was enjoying the sun, the ocean and the happy sounds of children playing in the swimming pool when I got my sixtieth rejection email from the one agent whom I was placing all my hopes on since she was among the rare ones specializing in spiritual fiction.

Sixtieth Literary Agent Rejection for *The Seeker*

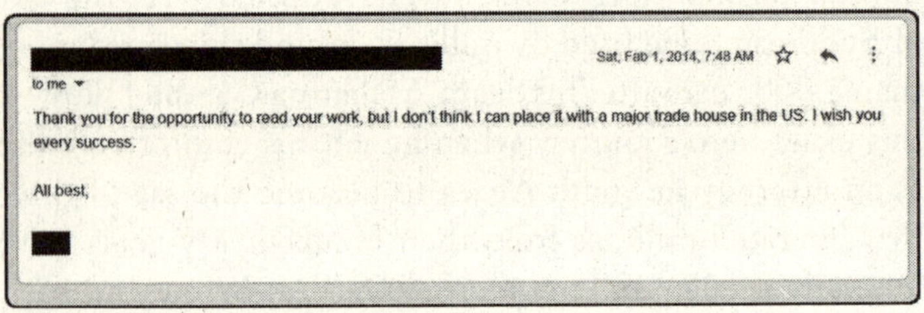
Sat, Feb 1, 2014, 7:48 AM

to me

Thank you for the opportunity to read your work, but I don't think I can place it with a major trade house in the US. I wish you every success.

All best,

Source: Provided by the author

I was dying inside while trying to keep a calm presence for my six-month-old daughter. I'd left my job to write and had nothing to show for it after eighteen months of non-stop effort. Was there ever a bigger failure than me? I decided to give up writing that day and look for a job. Then, I changed my mind again the next day and vowed not to give up until I was published.

Following each abyss, I transformed in unexpected, profound ways. After WhiteHat Jr, for instance, I plan to devote myself to public service for the rest of my life, given the sense of meaning I had in creating 12,000 teacher jobs from scratch. I'd never thought I would join the public sector, but the start-up journey made me realize that the 24x7 entrepreneurial energy of the private sector coming into the public sector can create millions of jobs and lead to unprecedented economic development. Now I want to live my dharma of impact at the largest possible level.

You too will transform from your hero's journey. You know your destiny from the exercise you did on the first page. This is your dharma. Do you hear the quiet call to adventure deep in your subconscious? This is your moment.

Now is your time. Use the rules in Part I and execution in Part II to cross the threshold into the unknown world and take the first step to live a life of your calling. One day, you'll return with the Gift of Goddess for all—and I'll be right here celebrating your journey!

Notes

Part 1: The 7 Rules for Freedom

Chapter 1: The 4 per cent Rule

1. William P. Bengen, 'Determining Withdrawal Rates Using Historical Data', *Journal of Financial Planning*, March 2004.
2. Table showing rolling return calculations (data sources are mentioned below the table):

	US			India	
Average Rolling Returns for 20 years as on 31 December 2021	**S&P 500**	**DJIA**	**Nasdaq 100**	**Sensex**	**BSE 500**
Price Returns					
3 yr	7.68%	7.01%	13.62%	15.50%	15.90%
5 yr	7.18%	6.83%	13.14%	14.02%	14.42%
7 yr	6.87%	6.45%	12.91%	12.74%	13.13%

10 yr	7.45%	6.96%	13.38%	12.26%	12.51%
15 yr	6.99%	6.69%	12.91%	13.65%	14.00%
Dividend Yield					
3 yr	1.96%	2.39%	0.82%	1.33%	1.35%
5 yr	2.00%	2.43%	0.85%	1.34%	1.34%
7 yr	2.01%	2.45%	0.87%	1.36%	1.35%
10 yr	2.01%	2.45%	0.89%	1.37%	1.36%
15 yr	2.00%	2.43%	0.85%	1.34%	1.34%
Inflation (CPI)					
	US			India	
3 yr	2.09%			6.93%	
5 yr	2.02%			7.15%	
7 yr	1.93%			7.44%	
10 yr	1.95%			7.62%	
15 yr	2.02%			7.13%	
Max Tax Rate (in 2022)					
	US			India	
Long-term Capital Gains Tax	20%			11.50%	
Dividends Tax	20%			41.10%	
Inflation Indexed, Post-Tax Returns					
3 yr	5.63%	5.43%	9.46%	7.57%	7.93%
5 yr	5.32%	5.38%	9.17%	6.05%	6.40%
7 yr	5.17%	5.18%	9.09%	4.64%	4.98%

10 yr	5.62%	5.58%	9.47%	4.04%	4.26%
15 yr	5.17%	5.27%	8.98%	5.74%	6.05%

Notes:

- Equity returns and dividend yields are based on Bloomberg data.
- India's Inflation values are from the Federal Reserve Bank of St Louis (Missouri, US).
- USA's Inflation values are from Yale University's page of Dr Robert J. Shiller (author of *Irrational Exuberance* [2000]).
- India tax data are from various newspapers and websites like ClearTax, PolicyBazaar.
- US tax data are based on official data on the IRS website and 'NerdWallet' articles.
- Rolling returns for 'price returns' are on a monthly basis, while for 'dividend yield' and 'inflation' these are on annual basis. For monthly basis, we calculated month-on-month returns and then averaged it for all the months of the time period to get the rolling return.

3. Ibid.
4. Ibid.
5. Ibid.

Chapter 2: Net Impact Rule

1. Joseph Epstein, 'Think You Have a Book in You? Think Again', *New York Times*, 28 September 2002.
2. James Scott Bell, 'What Is Plot, Anyway?', *Writer's Digest*, 24 September 2008.
3. George Land and Beth Jarman, *Breaking Point and Beyond*, HarperBusiness, 1993.
4. Kyril Kotashev, 'Start-up Failure Rate: How Many Start-ups Fail and Why?', Failory: The All-in-One Content Site

for Start-up Founders, 9 January 2022; Chris Anderson, 'A Bookselling Tail', *Publishers Weekly*, 14 July 2006.

5. Start-ups in India: Time to exit.

Industry	India Start-up Split (%)	Time to Exit (yr)
Enterprise Tech	15	9 yr
Health Tech	10	7
Ed Tech	9	7
FinTech	9	4
Retail Tech	7	5
Consumer Tech	6	5
HR Tech	6	9
Entertainment	4	7
Advertising	4	9
Logistics	3	NA
Others	28	NA
	Weighted Average Exit	6.96

Sources:

- Sanyukta Kanwal, 'Distribution of Start-ups in India 2020, by Sector' Statista.com, 16 March 2022.
- Sammy Abdullah, 'How Long Does It Take a Start-up to Exit?',About.crunchbase.com, 25 November 2018.

6. Amy Watson, 'Number of Publisher Rejections Before First Book Sale among Young Adult Authors in the United States as of September 2017', Statista, 18 February 2018.

Chapter 3: Salary/14 Lakh Quitting Rule

1. Marina Umaschi Bers, *Coding as a Playground: Programming and Computational Thinking in the Early Childhood Classroom*, Routledge, 2017.

2. First Transitions study and RedCore Consulting India study.
3. Tim Ferriss, 'Why You Should Define Your Fears Instead of Your Goals', TED Talk, 2017.

Chapter 4: '30×7' Ownership Shift

1. Based on analysis of fifteen major Multinational Corporations (MNCs) and their CEOs:

Company	CEO	Age when CEO
American Express	Stephen Squeri	59
Apple	Tim Cook	51
Michael Wirth	Chevron	57
Coca-Cola	James Quency	51
Walt Disney	Bob Chapek	60
Goldman Sachs	David Solomon	56
Honeywell	Darius Adamczyk	51
Dow Inc.	James Ray Fitterling	54
Procter & Gamble	Jon R. Moeller	57
Walmart	Carl Douglas McMillon	48
Twitter	Parag Agarwal	37
Microsoft	Satya Nadella	47
Amazon	Andy Jassy	53
CVS Health	Karen S. Lynch	58
United Health Group	Sir Andrew Philip Witty	57
Average age at CEO		**53**

Source: Google

Hence, assuming one begins a career after graduation at around 22–23 years of age, the average time taken to become a CEO is 53 – 23, i.e., thirty years.

Chapter 5: Your Daily '1,1,1' Routine

1. Verne Harnish, *Scaling Up: How a Few Companies Make It … And Why the Rest Don't:* CreateSpace Independent Publishing Platform, 2014.
2. Jeff Haden, 'A Study of 800 Million Activities Predicts Most New Year's Resolutions Will Be Abandoned on January 19: How to Create New Habits That Actually Stick', Inc.

Chapter 6: The '90 Per Cent Failing/100 Per Cent Learning' Rule

1. Paid television channels outcome analyses in India (2000–20):

S. No.	Channel Name	Launch Year	Paid/FTA	Status	Broadcaster	Existing Big Broadcaster Scale
11	&TV	2015	Paid	Running	Zee	Yes
22	Zee Next	2007	Paid	Shut (2009)	Zee	Yes
33	Zindagi	2014	Paid	Shut (2017)	Zee	Yes
44	Zee Smile	2004	Paid	Shut (2005)	Zee	Yes

55	Star One	2004	Paid	Shut (2011), Converted to LifeOK	Disney	Yes
66	Life OK	2011	Paid	Shut (2017), Converted to Star Bharat	Disney	Yes
77	Colors	2008	Paid	Running	Viacom	No
88	9X	2007	Paid	Shut (2015)	9X Media	No
99	Discovery Jeet	2017	Paid	Shut (2017)	Discovery	No
110	Imagine TV	2008	Paid	Shut (2014)	NDTV (Sold to Turner)	No
111	Real TV	2009	Paid	Shut (2010)	JV (Turner/ Alva Brothers)	No
112	Sahara One	2000	Paid	Shut (2015)	Sahara Media	No
113	Metro Gold	2000	Paid	Shut (2001)	JV (DD, 9 TV Network)	No

Notes:

- Overall, paid new television channels with original programming launched in the last two decades in India had a success rate of 15 per cent (2/13).
- Moderating for large network effect, where a new channel gets support from the parent network for advertising, the success rate falls to 8 per cent (1/13).

Source: Industry research

2. Tunia Cherian, '90% Start-ups in India Fail within 5 Years: IBM', *The Hindu Business Line*, 11 January 2018.
3. Anjelica Oswald, 'J.K. Rowling Shares Photos of Her Rejection Letters for "Inspiration"', *Business Insider*, 26 March 2016.
4. Brian Chesky, '7 Rejections', Medium, 13 July 2015.
5. Lata Jha, 'Indian families Still Watch TV Together: BARC', *Livemint*, 4 Oct 2018.
6. James Altucher, 'What I Learned about Life after Interviewing 80 Highly Successful People', James Altucher's Blog, available at jamesaltucher.com
7. Korn Ferry, 'Learning Agility: A Highly Prized Quality in Today's Marketplace', Focus: Get Your People Strategy Right, available at focus.kornferry.com

Chapter 7: '50/30/20' Investing Rule

1. Asit Manohar, 'How 50-30-20 Rule Helps You Meet Investment Goals', *Livemint*, 12 May 2021.
2. Bloomberg data on equity price returns and dividend yields combined shows 13 per cent returns on S&P 500 between 2010 and 2020.
3. The Federal Reserve Bank of St Louis data on US National Home Price Index, base January 2000 = 100, monthly, seasonally adjusted.
4. 'Why Equity over FDs, Gold and Real Estate?', IIFL Securities, available at indiainfoline.com
5. Based on Harry Markowitz, 'Portfolio Selection', *The Journal of Finance*, Vol. 7, No. 1 (1952), pp. 77–91.
6. In fact, as per Forbes, three largest target date fund providers—Fidelity, Vanguard and T. Rowe Price—hold much closer to '125—Your Age'. For example, these three target date funds allocate 90 per cent in stocks for a thirty-year-old, and about 75–85% in stocks for a fifty-year-old.
7. Eric Rosenberg, 'Most Investment Pros Can't Beat the Stock Market, So Why Do Everyday Investors Think They Can Win?', *Business Insider*, 1 August 2020.

8. Emmie Martin, 'Warren Buffett Recommends a Simple Exercise Before You Buy Any Stock: Write Down Your Why', CNBC, 24 February 2020.
9. Fidelity Viewpoints, 'The Guide to Diversification', Fidelity, 6 February 2022.

Part 2: Step-by-Step Ownership Kit

Introduction: Let's Get Started

1. US Bureau of Labour Statistics, *Employment by detailed occupation*. bls.gov.
2. CMIE Data (2019) suggests that of the 410 million working population, 76 million are self-employed. But 56 million of these 76 million are not entrepreneurs in true sense because they haven't been able to create employment for others. So, only 20 million or 5 per cent (of 410 million) are truly job creators in India.
3. Gallup, *State of the global workforce report: 2021 Report*. Gallup Press, 2021.

Chapter 9: Start-up Starter Kit Number 2

1. Sajith Pai, 'India2, English Tax and Building for the Next Billion Users', Medium, 13 June 2018.
2. Office of the Registrar General and Census Commissioner, India, 'HH-14 Households Having Children in the Age Group 5–14 Years by Number of Children Attending School', available at censusindia.gov.in
3. United Nations, Department of Economic and Social Affairs, Population Division, 'Household Size and Composition Around the World 2017—Data Booklet', United Nations: Economic and Social Affairs, available at https://www.un.org/en/development/desa/population/publications/pdf/ageing/

household_size_and_composition_around_the_world_2017_data_booklet.pdf
4. Execution ease for a particular country is based on a plethora of factors like language, regulation, cultural nuances, political climate, etc.
5. Kala Vijayraghavan, 'Unilever takes HUL strategies like small packs, cheaper variants to developed markets', Economictimes.indiatimes.com 28 September 2012.

Chapter 10: Start-up Starter Kit Number 3

1. Kim-Mai Cutler, 'Lessons from a Study of Perfect Pitch Decks: VCs Spend an Average of 3 Minutes, 44 Seconds on Them', TechCrunch, 8 June 2015.
2. Sridharan Gunasekaran at intake@slidemarvels.com.
3. Jitesh Agarwal at Treelife: jitesh@treelife.in.

Chapter 11: Start-up Starter Kit Number 5

1. Ralph Benko, 'Peter Thiel: "We Don't Live in a Normal World; We Live Under a Power Law"', Forbes, 13 October 2014.
2. Ibid.
3. Tim Ferriss, *Tribe Of Mentors: Short Life Advice from the Best in the World*: HarperCollins, 2017.
4. Paul Graham, *Hackers & Painters: Big Ideas from the Computer Age* (Newton, Massachusetts: O'Reilly Media, 2004).

Chapter 13: Start-up Starter Kit Number 6

1. 'What is Net Promoter Score®? Your introduction to NPS', Hotjar, 2 February 2022, available at hotjar.com
2. 'A Deep Dive into the Anatomy of Premature Scaling', Start-up Genome, 2 September 2011, available at www.start-upgenome.com

Acknowledgments

KERRY, my wife, kept believing in me through the turbulence of starting from scratch multiple times and changing locations, industries and careers often in the last decade of following our paths. Her support pulled me through many moments of self-doubt along the way.

Our daughters, Leela and Rumi, have lived off a backpack and little stuff for most of their lives—I love them deeply for their big, adventurous and flexible spirits.

My father, late mother and my sister, Sonali, have been very big-hearted and supportive in always letting me march to the tune of my own drum. As have my grandmother, aunt, Madhu Arora, and the Bajajs.

I want to thank everyone at WhiteHat Jr who kept steadfast belief in me through the ups and downs of this once-in-a-lifetime '30X7' journey. There are too many outstanding folks to recognize fully here but just a word for those who took the leap of faith early and shaped the company as much as I did: Sini George, Anurag Shukla, Gauri Parulkar, Dr Farida Khan, Abhijeet Gawande, Rahul

Dagariya, Nikhil Mittal, Pranab Dash, Pratik Vimal, Swati Ganeti, Thomas Lagashu, Suyash Tyagi, Sapna Pandey, Trupti Mukker. My early investors, Anup Gupta from Nexus, Siddharth Nautiyal, Sarvesh Kanodia, and Namita Dalmia from Omidyar and Amit Patel from Owl, will always have a special place in my heart for trusting me when I had little more than a power-point presentation. I also have deep admiration for Byju Raveendran's single-minded devotion to changing the nature of learning for kids all over the world.

I was fortunate to get inputs on the book from many close friends who were tremendously helpful with their detailed edits: Trupti Mukker, Jitesh Agarwal, Garima Mitra, Sai Abhishek, Pratibha Jain, Dushyant Singh, Issac John, Saurabh Nanda, Vivekanand Tripathi, Sanjay Singh, Vinod Raghuvanshi, Nideesh Vasu, and Claire Senac.

Matthew Sharpe was an incredibly thoughtful early editor and helped shape the book. Anupam Anand, RedCore and Praveen Chaudhary were very meticulous in doing deep quantitative and qualitative research to substantiate various points made in the book. Ruth Alarcon and Nare Arshakyan did the graphics and formats with their usual panache.

Sachin Sharma from HarperCollins India is a dream publisher with his deep knowledge of the industry and his superb champion spirit. The book is also richer for Pooja Sanyal's excellent editing and HarperCollins India's commitment from Ananth Padmanabhan's always-extraordinary vision to the marketing team's detailed launch plan.

Finally, a note of gratitude to the readers of *Keep Off The Grass, Johnny Gone Down* and *The Seeker,* as well as my YouTube channel and blog. I've been sporadic in my content, only writing things that deeply mattered to me when they mattered, yet you've followed each endeavour with the same enthusiastic energy. You've inspired me to keep experimenting and come closer and closer to what's true.

About the Author

Karan Bajaj is the founder of WhiteHat Jr, acquired by BYJU's, among the fastest exits of its size in India. He's also a bestselling novelist whose books have sold more than 150,000 copies in India and optioned for movie deals: *Keep Off the Grass* (2008), *Johnny Gone Dow*n (2010), published by HarperCollins, *The Seeker* (2015), and *The Yoga of Max's Discontent* (2016), published by Penguin Random House. A graduate of IIM-Bangalore and BIT Mesra, Karan has earlier served as the head of Discovery Networks in India. Also a striving yogi, Karan has taken three year-long career sabbaticals to pursue his interests in spirituality, writing and hiking.

Please reach out to Karan here if you ever get stuck on your path to freedom.

Email: karan@karanbajaj.com

Blog: http://www.karanbajaj.com/

LinkedIn: https://www.linkedin.com/in/karan-bajaj- 8806191

YouTube: https://www.youtube.com/c/KaranBajajOfficial

